The Timeless
Time Machine

The Timeless Time Machine

Jay Dubya

www.bookstandpublishing.com

Published by
Bookstand Publishing
Pasadena, CA 91101
4934_2

ISBN 978-1-956785-28-9

For Joe and Dan

Other Books by Jay Dubya

Adult Fiction

Black Leather and Blue Denim, A '50s Novel
The Great Teen Fruit War, A 1960' Novel
Frat' Brats, A '60s Novel
Ron Coyote, Man of La Mangia
Pieces of Eight
Pieces of Eight, Part II
Pieces of Eight, Part III
Pieces of Eight, Part IV
The Wholly Book of Genesis
The Wholly Book of Exodus
The Wholly Book of Doo-Doo-Rot-on-Me
Thirteen Sick Tasteless Classics
Thirteen Sick Tasteless Classics, Part II
Thirteen Sick Tasteless Classics, Part III
Thirteen Sick Tasteless Classics, Part IV
Thirteen Sick Tasteless Classics, Part V
So Ya' Wanna' Be A Teacher
RAM: Random Articles and Manuscripts
Mauled Maimed Mangled Mutilated Mythology
Fractured Frazzled Folk Fables and Fairy Farces
FFFF&FF, Part II
Nine New Novellas
Nine New Novellas, Part II
Nine New Novellas, Part III
Nine New Novellas, Part IV
One Baker's Dozen
Two Baker's Dozen
Shakespeare: Slammed, Smeared, Savaged & Slaughtered
Shakespeare: Slammed, Smeared, Savaged & Slaughtered, Part II
Suite 16
Time Travel Tales
Snake Eyes and Boxcars
Snake Eyes and Boxcars, Part II
UFO: Utterly Fantastic Occurrences

Young Adult Fantasy Novels

Content Chapters

Introduction

The *Timeless Time Machine* is adult satirical literature featuring adult language and adult situations. The setting is London, England, 1899, at the turn of a new century, and the exciting advances of science and technology are dominant in the minds of people throughout the Western World.

Herbert George Wells (1866-1946) was born in England, and by the turn of the century, became one of the Founding Fathers of science fiction. Wells' most famous novels are *The Time Machine*, *War of the Worlds*, and *The Invisible Man*, which were written and published between 1895 and 1905.

H.G. Wells was a great student of history, and loved thinking about mankind's ultimate destiny. In his stories, Wells often tells through his characters what *he* believes is wrong with civilization, so that's why the author never ran out of characters for his popular novels. By mentally taking his readers into the future, Herbert George Wells skillfully demonstrates exactly where the human race would be evolving unless science, culture, and emotional growth change their present courses. Herein lies a new, adult-oriented, satirical version of H.G. Wells' short classic novel, *The Time Machine*.

Chapter 1

"THE TIME MACHINE"

I have been a casual acquaintance of the Time Traveler (for that's what he is presently calling himself all the hell over London) for many years. The T.T. habitually had a group of friends assemble inside his dining room each Thursday evening at his pleasant home in Richmond, a nice, pleasant section of London, that was later disassembled and moved to Virginia, just like the widely acclaimed *London Bridge* had been dismantled, and then transported and later reconstructed in Arizona.

I stared at the Time Traveler's ashen face and thought, 'Who the fuck smeared ashes all over your' damned face?' But I was too timid to make my secret contemplation known to my eminent colleagues. That evening, our host's gray eyes twinkled like little stars, and I noticed that his hand and head gesticulations were more animated than usual.

My eyes glanced around the dining room and observed that the hearth-fire was blazing-away inside the fireplace, ever since our host had thrown his dirty underwear into it, and as my eyes scanned my fellow listeners seated at *his* familiar table after enjoying a fine mutton dinner, the Time Traveler began telling the most extraordinary story I believe I had ever heard him narrate, or anyone else, ever verbally relate. Most of us were too flabbergasted to openly challenge our host's rather-convincing veracity.

"You corpulent, guest-numbskulls must follow my graphic description carefully," the Time Traveler pragmatically began his exposition. "Because after I say a few words, I can't at all seem to remember the rest of my introduction. I regret that this memory loss to which I allude is a problem that most creative and inventive people apparently have and share, and I'm no damned exception. I tend to occasionally lose my train of thought, locomotive, caboose, everything!"

"Thank goodness we're all not creative and inventive like you are," the usually-pessimistic Medical Man criticized. "Or else, nobody here would ever be able to recollect what the fuck *you* ever said."

"What the Medical Man is attempting to convey," Blank, the newspaper Editor, diplomatically interrupted, "is that *we* understand your words perfectly and correctly, but we can never seem to fathom the ideas that the ludicrous descriptions represent. I mean, there's a reason why my name is Blank!"

"I agree," enthusiastically admitted the garrulous Time Traveler, "that the more words one knows in his or her vocabulary, the harder it is for him or her to communicate with all of the assholes whom he or she comes into contact. It's like a weird disconcerting conundrum. But in the matter which I'm about to disclose," our knowledgeable clever host continued, "I shall challenge several basic concepts that you assembled dolts almost universally endorse. For example," the Time Traveler cited, "the lousy Euclidian geometry that you had learned in school is as false as tissue paper stuffed inside a flat-chested prostitute's brassiere, which she has been advertising as nice firm tits."

"Isn't that a large chunk of bullshit to expect us to begin upon?" asked Filby, an argumentative red-haired rebel, who habitually persisted in puncturing everybody's scrotum, and then randomly breaking their delicate balls thereafter. "Are you being facetious while fabricating another absurd allegory?" the retail store owner asked.

"I don't expect you *to believe* every word out of my mouth, because I'm not starting a goddamned religion here," the Time Traveler maintained. "You, Filby, my good neighbor, will soon agree to as much as I need from you to understand; so therefore, forget about your propensity for castrating your friends' rear ends and kissing your enemies' butts, which are your most obvious bad traits. Now then," the Time Traveler proceeded after ascertaining that he had finally achieved gaining *our* undivided attention, "you all are aware that a mathematical line has no thickness, and no real existence. That arithmetical principle had been erroneously taught to you in school."

"That statement is quite true," answered the renowned Psychologist sitting to my left. "That idea you've just mentioned is a pure abstraction that's never really lost its virginity. It's just as axiomatic in life as is the existence of psychopaths, sociopaths, and the abundant whorehouse paths all over London! Ha, ha, ha!"

"And a cube," the Time Traveler resumed his discourse while ignoring the rest of us indulgently laughing our asses off, "can a three-dimensional cube having only length, breadth, and height really have any actual abstract existence? I don't think so!"

"On that I beg to differ with you," commented and chuckled Filby. "Certainly, solid objects like a nice pair of firm tits, or a humongous erection, can exist in three dimensions. All real things…"

"So, that's what most people wrongly think," the Time Traveler adamantly trumped Filby with his superior command of the English language. "But just wait a freakin' moment. Can an *instantaneous* cube exist?"

"Not when it dissolves quickly in hot coffee or tea!" Blank, the empty-headed Editor remarked and loudly laughed, and we all boisterously joined his absurd merriment, except for the very serious Time Traveler, who was getting more and more pissed-off by our general whimsical jocularity. "We aren't dumb-ass religious disciples, so we just don't follow you!" Blank punned and admitted. "We aren't fuckin' lost little puppy dogs that gotta' obediently follow you, either, ya' know. Ha, ha, ha! Arf, arf, arf!"

"Obviously," the perturbed Time Traveler answered, biting his tongue and then solemnly proceeding to deliver his austere lecture. "Any real body must have extension in *four* basic directions."

"Head, arms, legs and dick?" Filby idiotically chortled as the rest of us guffawed like clamorous spectators at a raunchy Leatherhead burlesque show for leather-headed jerk-offs. "That fourth direction I've just mentioned is a real stretch! Ha, ha, ha!"

"No, you pathetic Asshole!" the Time Traveler vehemently admonished our red-haired friend. "Filby," *he* emphasized and gesticulated. "Everything visible and existing in the material world, even Lady Madonna, who owns the neighborhood Richmond Sex Toy and S and M Pleasure Company, must have length, breadth, thickness and duration."

"Everything except a hard-on!" the Psychologist (a Freudian psychologist at that) butted-in. "An erection definitely has length, breadth and thickness, but its duration is for a maximum of ten brief minutes of thrusting and pumping. It's only temporary and not permanent."

"Exactly!" the slightly-aggravated Time Traveler amazingly concurred with the insane Psychologist. "You hit the gorilla right in the balls. There are really only three observable dimensions that your charlatan math' teachers had taught you in school, and that you had fallaciously learned in geometry class. The three planes of space: length, breadth and thickness. But…"

"I hated geometry in school," the grumpy Editor openly confessed and interrupted. "And now that the adolescent horseshit is all behind me, I'm certainly happy for experiencing the after*math.* "

"Tell us more about this geometry crock of feces!" ballbreaker Filby encouraged our cordial host. "After all, you've generously fed us a decent meal, and now it's our assumed obligation to listen to your frivolous, theatrical, happy horse manure."

"As I was attempting to say," the stubborn Time Traveler uttered, gritting his teeth, "the first three dimensions of physical space move in a parallel manner with us from birth to death, and we generally take *their* accompaniment for granted. But gentlemen," the remarkable local inventor continued his preposterous lecture, "I submit to you that the fourth dimension is merely what we casually call 'time'. It does not travel in the same direction as length, breadth and thickness do, but invisible *time* exists almost perpendicular to those three other standard geometric dimensions. You've all heard what mathematicians have said about the *Fourth Dimension* haven't you?"

"That they're an excellent singing band, almost as good and as talented as the *Sixth Dimension?*" Filby laughed as the nutcase alluded to an imaginary 1895 singing group.

"I've not heard or read any significant bullshit about the *Fourth Dimension*, nor do I care to hear or read about it!" the petulant and cantankerous Provincial Mayor exclaimed. "It's all a lot of poppycock, you know!"

"That an invisible *Fourth Dimension* called *time* exists at right angles proportionate to the standard three dimensions of ordinary plane geometry," the Time Traveler seriously disclosed as if he were embarking on the exploration of a new revolutionary theorem. "Do you lowbrow idiots see what the fuck I mean? Are you all honor graduates from Dunce University?"

"I think so," grunted the peeved Provincial Mayor, who couldn't stop farting both out of his ass and out of his mouth. "I think so!" the dumb-shit politician answered as the egomaniac lapsed into a rare introspective state where he wasn't (for a change) daydreaming about horny hookers or female nudist colonies for dimwitted voyeurs like himself peering into binoculars. "Yes, I think I see your marvelous theory, becoming tangible now, flourishing beyond its initial abstraction stage!"

"Well, I must inform you, my distinguished Neanderthal guests, that I've been studying and experimenting with this four-dimension business for quite some time," the Time Traveler rather-dramatically revealed. "Now, please for argument's sake, kindly direct your scrutiny to this common weather chart I've diligently prepared. Notice how the barometer rises and falls from day to day, just like Filby's disobedient pecker does. Yesterday, it was this high; last night it was down to here, and this morning the barometer/temperature reading rose-up to seventy degrees Fahrenheit. Now the imaginary line your trained minds are presently tracing represents the path of mercury level rising or falling from day to day," the Time Traveler editorialized. "That abstract connection which your feeble brains are currently associating is the *time line*, or what contemporary theoretical scientists are presently calling the basic introduction to the *Fourth Dimension!*"

"Can't you show us something more palpable and graphic like nude women with opened, spread-eagle beavers, or kinky photos' of two lesbians inserting massive dildos up each other's wet, pink, hairy snatcheroos'," the demented Freudian Psychologist insisted. "Get with the goddamned program, Mr. Wells. My post-dinner appetite demands something more entertaining."

"But," the usually sarcastic Medical Man injected while staring hard at the blazing fireplace flames, wishing that he were just as hot while massaging the chest of a big-tit hussy. "If time is nothing more than the fourth dimension of what we call 'space', why can't we move about in time as we do in length, breadth and thickness; that is, move the same way we can when we get laid, or when we jerk-off, whenever we can't get laid. Thank God for straight kinky women, that's all' the fuck I have to say!" the lunatic Medical Man elaborated and exaggerated. "I'd never let a goddamned lesbian suck my precious stiff private; never, I say."

The prudent Time Traveler smiled at his doubting dissenters. "Are you sure you can move around liberally in space? Right and left you can go, and backward and forward, but that covers only two of the three standard dimensions. What about up and down?" the Time Traveler questioned his totally puzzled audience. "Gravity definitely limits our mobility in that tricky third dimension situation."

"Look neighbor!" Filby objected. "As long as my pecker can rivet like a hyperactive piston up and down for six inches at a thrust, I don't give a fuck about height or thickness. or whatever the hell ya' wanna' call it; even if that third-dimension limits me while I'm vigorously pumpin' away!"

"But there are flying balloons with gondolas under them that can overcome this limitation of up and down that *you,* my gregarious host, had in the past called gravity," the pensive Medical Man academically presented. "Has anybody here ever had sex in a merry up-up-and-away, beautiful hot air balloon yet?"

"But before the invention of the hot air balloon," the Time Traveler argued above the abundant laughter and giggling, "man had little or no freedom of vertical movement, other than climbing a ladder, or falling out of a damned tree. Do you big-bellied imbeciles comprehend what the hell I'm saying here?"

"Look!" the blunt Medical Man yelled, out-of-character; getting everyone's immediate attention. "Nobody can move around in time. It's fuckin' crazy to even consider the foolish hypothesis. People move in one straight line," the renowned Doctor asserted from his daily experience and from his knowledge of inevitable death. "They're born; they live, and then they die, and all three fuckin' things happen to be going in the same damned direction."

"My dear Doctor, that is where both you and the entire academic world are entirely and absolutely wrong," the Time Traveler maintained. "True, our mental cognizance of our relationship to our environment is passing along the time line to which *you* have accurately alluded from the cradle to the grave. But," our illustrious host pointed-out, "I've discovered that it's possible to remove oneself from the present, and either journey back into history, or venture into the distant future, whichever happens to interest my fancy."

"You're definitely fucked-up, and genuine insane asylum material!" Filby screamed at our extremely intelligent-but-very-eccentric host. "You're even more totally fucked-up than our mutual friend the Freudian Psychologist is!"

"To my knowledge, gentlemen, negative thinking never either invented or created anything! Now, to appease you very diffi*cult* agnostics and dubious apostates," the Time Traveler articulated, "movement in the *Fourth Dimension* constitutes the very essence of my great discovery. Let's say that I'm presently recalling screwing my seventy-year-old-fiancee last night. My mind flashes back to the instant of that non-sensational occurrence. I become absent-minded, so to speak," our ingenious host insisted. "Then, my wandering mind returns to the present, and I must look at you pathetic morons, and suddenly, I wish I was back to last night pumping the poop out of my dry-well, seventy-year-old promiscuous fiancée."

"A civilized man is far better-off than a mere savage, or an uneducated aborigine is," Filby proposed, completely out of context and off the subject. "Because a modern man has science, and can screw on mattresses with springs in them; whereas, primitive cannibals and barbarians have to pump their women on hard surfaces. But in the final analysis," Filby humorously argued, "your fascinating theory is a bunch of irrelevant bullshit, unless of course, *you* can amply demonstrate its application, preferably with six beautiful naked ladies in heat."

"Filby's absolutely right," the Freudian Psychologist declared. "You can show black is white by shrewd argument, but you can only wipe your smelly ass in the present time. And besides, who would just want to go to the past or to the future and watch other people wiping their smelly assholes? Ha, ha, ha!"

"Long ago, I planned manufacturing a revolutionary, breakthrough machine," the beleaguered Time Traveler shouted above the excessive laughter *we* were generating. "It would be a marvelous machine that transcended the limitations of gravity, and would supersede the limitations of the first three already-discussed dimensions. Gentlemen," the Time Traveler carefully and seriously stated. "I have meticulously designed and constructed a workable model of an apparatus that could easily journey through time, and then return to the present with its operator seated aboard."

"Why the hell don't you just invent something practical like a better mousetrap than something crazy like a fanciful, stupid-assed, fantasy time machine?" Filby angrily challenged. "Ya' can't catch any mice with a dumb-assed imaginary time machine!"

The Time Traveler ignored Filby's preposterous diatribe and attested, "I have experimental proof to substantially verify my claim!"

"This bizarre time machine thing could definitely come in handy," the Editor speculated while considering some practical applications for the device that *his* pleasure-oriented mind was imagining. "Let's say my wife is returning early from the gynecologist's office, and wants to get laid after getting a clean bill-of-health for her snatcheroo from the cross-eyed, love-tunnel doctor. Imagine this scenario I'm describing. Unfortunately, I'm home in my bedroom initiating sex with a gorgeous lady reporter in my employ when my horny wife enters the house and dashes up the steps to get it on!"

"Why not just have a threesome going to solve your hypothetical crisis?" Filby constructively inquired. "The year 1899 is no time to be prudish. I mean, even Queen Victoria is showing a little more leg and chest than she did only forty short years ago!"

"Stop interrupting my train of thought, Filby!" the Editor volleyed-back to the well-known local instigator/aggravator. "Now, as I was saying," the newspaper man proceeded with his speculation. "If I had a Time Machine, my girlfriend and I could just escape to another time, let's say the year 2003, and achieve our orgasms there without my desperate, horny wife ever suspecting that I was getting laid in the exact same place in another century. The prospects and benefits associated with me owning such a wonderful machine are rather fascinating, to say the least! Manufacture one for me, Mr. Wells, and I'll gladly buy it at any reasonable price!"

"You have no freight cars on your silly train of thought," the cynical Medical Man criticized the Editor. "Only a stupid-assed loco-motive!"

"Not only that," the perverted Freudian Psychologist added, ignoring the ridiculous argument transpiring between the Medical Doctor and the newspaper Editor. "The use of such a terrific machine would do *me* no good. Let's say I'm porking my blonde maid like I usually do, when all of a sudden, my nosy wife surprisingly comes home early from shopping for used sanitary napkins. If I take-off in the time machine with my beautiful lady employee," the Psychologist theorized and suggested, "my suspicious spouse will notice that neither I, nor the maid, is anywhere inside the house, and then the greedy and presumptuous bitch would promptly sue me for suspected adultery."

"But, if you were as smart as the average cockroach," Filby replied to the neurotic Freudian Psychologist, "you'd simply just stay in the Year 2003 with your luscious blonde maid and escape an expensive 1899 domestic lawsuit. Just remember to take along plenty of cash on your time travel voyage, along with all your redeemable stock certificates!"

"Yes, I see where I could very practically use Mr. Wells' marvelous advanced transportation device," the extremely-perverted, pedophile Freudian Psychologist acknowledged. "When needed in an emergency, a functional Time Machine could also be a convenient Sex Machine!"

"A Time Machine would be an exceptionally-valuable device for an historian," the Editor constructively contributed to the bizarre conversation. "A researcher could travel back to the *Battle of Hastings* in 1066, and prove that it actually had happened as our history textbooks state it did. Or better yet," the psyched-up newspaper mogul added. "I could go back to ancient Greece, and visit the Isle of Lesbos, and watch all the lesbians getting off on one another. God! Do I love an erect squiggly clitoris and fellas', nothing turns me on more than squiggly clitorises!" the sex-crazed, perverted, hedonistic, mental-case Editor elaborated. "As a certified registered voyeur, I could appreciate and confirm all the wonderful abnormal sex that had transpired in the lyric gay poetess' Sapphos' residence on Lesbos. And a whole room full of fabulous squiggly clitorises, with honey-sweet-wet-pink-hairy pussies, would be enough to make me blast a heavy load of semen out of my throbbing dingle, and send the discharge right though a solid marble statue of Aphrodite!"

"Wow!" Filby marveled and exclaimed, faking being impressed. "There were lesbians and homosexuals in ancient Greece thousands of years before the gay nineties? Why that's absolutely incredible! Say, didn't Aphrodite run a prosperous baby diaper service in Egypt?"

"And also," added the dull and formerly reticent Economics Professor, who always took pride in ruining our obnoxious frivolity.

"Just think gentlemen! An individual could invest all of his money in the year 1899, and then speed ahead in his unique Time Machine to 2003; collect his accumulated interest; do comprehensive research in a library, and then bet all his dough on horse races and sporting events in the year 1899," the academic wizard chuckled. "A person could easily amass a fabulous fortune and become the richest man in the whole goddamned world, simply by playing a sort of time ping-pong game by bouncing back and forth from century to century, and doing simple investing and gambling."

"You egocentric, self-centered assholes are nothing more than a human herd of selfish, conceited piss-heads!" the Time Traveler angrily bellowed in a thunderous voice. "What I've painstakingly created transcends your dumb-ass biological pleasure cravings! I've diligently invented this splendid machine for historical research purposes, and also to gain knowledge about the evolution of Earth civilizations," our host admonished his arrogant, narcissistic guests. "I want to establish safeguards against mankind stupidly self-destructing ourselves, and here all you dumb hiney-biters want to do is watch ancient lesbians lick each other's hairy slits, or escape getting caught by your wives while having baser-instinct-oriented, extra-marital affairs. What kind of goddamned ingrate, shit-head friends do I have, anyway?"

A moment of silence followed the indignant Time Traveler's well-deserved criticism. "The experiment," said all-too-skeptical Filby. "Let's see this idiotic, goddamned Time Machine experiment you had promised to show us before I need to be admitted to Bedlam, if St. Mary of Bethlehem admits my disheveled ass!"

"Yes, let's see your supposedly excellent demonstration," the egotistical Editor sarcastically commented in defense of Filby's reasonable demand. "Let's see it, even if it's all a lot of illogical humbug."

"Thank you, Ebenezer Scrooge!" the Time Traveler answered the self-indulgent irritator with a contrived smile. "As you all well-know, I'm a man of history, as well as one who advocates the advancement of science."

The Time Traveler then rose from his comfortable chair and placed his hands inside his trouser' pockets while searching for a particular key. Then, Mr. Wells nonchalantly whistled and shuffled his way down the long, narrow, drafty corridor toward his secluded playroom laboratory.

"I wonder what this Time Machine thing looks like?" the Freudian Psychologist asked while raising his eyebrows with an inquisitive expression showing upon his grim-looking face. "I hope the box is pink and wet, and looks like my paramour's box, and not like my wife's smelly pussy cave!"

"I'm sure it's some sort of magician's sleight-of-hand trick, comparable to one I recently saw given by a prestidigitator over in Mayfair," the Medical Man conjectured and opined. "I never quite figured-out how the conjurer did it. He made a Doberman pinscher's exquisite dick disappear right off the bottom of the cur's body, and now the poor de-peckered canine spends all night howling, and all day barking up the wrong tree, searching for its cherished missing sperm-shooter."

Before the zany Medical Man could finish his fairly-humorous oration, the Time Traveler returned from his brief expedition down the drafty, narrow hallway, holding a glistening metallic box in his hands. The fascinating object was no larger than an average-sized table clock, and the gleaming mechanism appeared very intricately configured. Some ivory parts, and a peculiar crystalline material seemed to be two of the principal materials from which it had been made.

The Time Traveler grabbed a corner chair and sat-down at the oval dining room table, upon which our host gently deposited the very attractive object. The only other items upon the table were a small dimly-lit shade lamp, and the Editor's snot-clogged handkerchief. A dozen or so candles were flickering around the dim room, some of them on tables, and several more in sconces situated on the walls and also above the fireplace mantel, so that the general room was more than moderately illuminated.

I maneuvered my chair and sat closest to the fireplace. I wanted to get a more accurate view of any phenomenon or irregularity that might happen. All of our eyes gazed upon the Time Traveler's determined countenance, and the perceptive spectators all impatiently waited for his descriptive preface. I was absolutely certain that a hoax could easily be identified with so many reliable eyewitnesses being present, and certainly, with such satisfactory, observational conditions prevailing.

"Well?" the Freudian Psychologist impulsively slipped with his tongue. "Maybe our extraordinary host can put my ulcers and my gout into that damned thing and make them miraculously disappear!"

"This delicate mechanism," the Time Traveler explained while fondling the thing as if it was a throbbing, squiggly, rubbery clitoris. "It's an authentic model of the actual Time Machine, but it's very capable of achieving a comparable function. It's my creative plan, gentlemen, for this intricate small unit to travel through time. You'll notice," the persuasive speaker said while indicating with his forefinger, "that it appears somewhat askew and surreal, and that its tiny controls sparkle and glitter. Notice these two small, white levers located side by side upon the instrument panel," Mr. Wells anxiously lectured, while showing us the unique ivory handles. "The one on the left will transport the imaginary passenger into the past, and the one on the right is calibrated to convey the rider speeding into the future."

"It's beautifully assembled!" the impressed Medical Man lavishly praised while examining the fantastic model, closely inspecting it through his monocle. "How much time did the bloody thing require, that is, all the way from the blueprint stage to the finished product?"

"It took me exactly two laborious years to build," the Time Traveler proudly related. "Kindly notice that besides the two-time levers, there is also a saddle in the center, which represents the seat that a time trekker would utilize. Have a good final examination of my stellar creation gentlemen, and ascertain that all possibility of deception has been eliminated. I don't want to fuckin' squander this complex model on a wasted experiment, and then be labeled as a certified wacky lunatic, ready for a bed in the nearest mental asylum!"

A momentary hush existed inside the dining room. A pin dropping, or even the most-quiet fart could have been easily discerned by *our* alert-but-suspicious ears. The apprehensive Freudian Psychologist was about to speak, but then wisely, bit his tongue. The Time Traveler took the paranoid Freudian Psychologist's finger to signify that our host didn't want the famous mind expert to become a *Fraudian* Psychologist. "Here Sir, add to the suspense. You do us the honor!" our host politely directed.

So, it was the perverted Freudian Psychologist that sent the remarkable miniature apparatus on its mysterious and ephemeral mission. We all saw the lever turn and then lock. We all observed the tiny machine pulsate and glow, and then there was a distinct blast of wind, and the candle flames in the wall sconces leaped-about, and then wildly flickered. The tiny machine was glowing and pulsating red and blue light, and in a matter of seconds, the incredible device appeared as a faint glimmer, wildly eddying around. And finally, the arcane mechanism vanished as if it were never lying there on the table, directly before our astonished eyes. The only things left upon the surface were the dimly-lit shade lamp, and the Editor's stenchy, snot-filled handkerchief.

"What the fuck happened?" the addled Medical Man shouted. "Where did the blasted thing disappear to?"

The Psychologist recovered from his temporary paralysis and stuck his bald head under the table, searching for some trace of the missing metallic cube. "There must be an element of fuckin' trickery associated with this uncanny exhibition?" the behavioral analyst disgustedly ranted. "There's nothing tangible under the damned table, except three suggestive gay porno' magazines, and a stack of nude pictures of the Royal Family!"

The Time Traveler chuckled at *our* apparent frustration. Mr. Wells was indeed, at that very moment, the absolute master of his environment. Then, the moody Medical Man had to annoyingly open his big fat mouth. "Are you sincere in what you've just shown us?"

the astounded physician earnestly asked our sometimes-facetious host. "Do you actually believe that your model has ventured into infinity? Did it go into the past, or into the future?"

"You're really an unobservant, incompetent, dysfunctional dumb-ass!" the terse Editor more-than-weakly criticized his weekly Thursday acquaintance. "Doctor; the Psychologist had his finger on the *right* lever, so obviously, the damned time machine model vanished into the future? Do you have a bad case of attention deficit syndrome, or what? You must be mentally challenged! Were you ever enrolled in special education, slow-learner classes?" the all-too-frank Editor chided the Medical Man.

"Gentlemen," the Time Traveler alertly interrupted the gaggle of non-illustrious disputers. "I have a larger, even more spectacular edition of the Time Machine that an adult could ride, and it's situated in the middle of my secret laboratory at the end of my narrow, drafty hallway. And when *that* apparatus is fully assembled," the Time Traveler divulged to his thoroughly-bewildered guests, "I intend to make my first monumental journey out of the year 1899."

The entire dining party sat there in the dim light, in an absolute stupor, staring at the vacant table for at least two full minutes. 'That weird thing disappeared faster than my money does!' I mentally concluded.

"It all seems remotely plausible enough this evening," the always-dubious Medical Man orally concluded. "But the common sense of tomorrow morning will fuckin' bring us all back to our trained occupational ways, and what we had witnessed here tonight will be just a faint memory of an inexplicable ruse. But still, right now," the totally confused Doctor stated, "I can't fuckin' explain the manifestation we all have just witnessed!"

"Look, if you think what you had seen with your own damned eyes was a cruel canard," the Time Traveler boomed at the befuddled Doctor, "then follow me down to my laboratory right now so that I can dispel any doubts floating around inside your negative mini-mind!"

Jay Dubya

The Time Traveler led his entourage down the narrow, drafty corridor, and then dramatically hesitated before opening the door to his isolated laboratory. The entry portal squeaked open on its rusty hinges, and inside the room we beheld a larger version of the model that had mysteriously disappeared in the dining room. The beautiful object flickered on and off, as the lit candles in the wall sconces seemed to accentuate and enhance the awesome object's pulsations. Parts that had been made of ivory, nickel, bronze, and sawn quartz crystal glowed red, to green, to violet, as if some sinister alien radiation was being emitted from the unearthly-looking time travel vehicle.

"Look here," the volatile Medical Man balked to the calm-in-demeanor Time Traveler. "You have a reputation around London for playing colossal tricks and pranks! Is this a goddamned bamboozle like that scary *Christmas ghost* you had projected upon the parlor wall last December 24th! I fuckin' hate phony flimflams, and I fuckin' hate being hoodwinked by exploitive con-artists! It makes me feel so inferior and so small every time some smart-alecky bastard like you tricks my ass!"

"I shall sit in the leather saddle upon my wonderful machine," the Time Traveler matter-of-factly predicted, "and I intend to explore history, and then advance on schedule into the far future. Do I make myself perfectly clear?"

None of us dared say a word, or even a syllable or a consonant. I could hear the Medical Man, the Editor, the Economics Professor, the Psychologist, Filby and myself gasping for air in the poorly-ventilated, "science-fiction chamber". No one in the fascinating experimental room even felt like thinking about sex, let alone about lustfully having it. Then, I heard the Psychologist sneeze in response to an allergy attack, which was automatically followed by a loud fart produced by the old fart's big fat ass.

"The actual Time Machine will be finished and ready for use later this week!" the Time Traveler passively-and-confidently informed us. "Then, I plan to return here to Richmond by next Thursday, and I'll divulge to you at dinner everything about my splendid and thrilling adventure into the future!"

Jay Dubya

Chapter 2

"LATE FOR DINNER"

I think that at that time, none of us quite believed in the Time Machine, or placed too much credence in the Time Traveler's "absurd claims". The fact is, the Time Traveler was one of those men who exaggerates, prevaricates, and plays imaginative tricks, and basically, Herbert George is entirely too clever to be believed: I never felt that everyone who attended those Thursday night dinners saw all around our weekly "Master of Ceremonies", especially last week, when our host spoke of the fourth dimension, since inventor Wells had a unique four-dimensional personality unlike anyone else that I've even known. And also, his weird, seemingly fucked-up ideas, besides being quite outlandish, were drastically difficult to fathom and fully comprehend.

I had always suspected that some subtle reserve, a certain energy indeed dwelled inside his scheming demeanor. Actually, Wells possessed some dynamic ingenuity in how he would ambush his audience, with his true personality camouflaged behind his external, lucid frankness. Had Filby shown the model and explained the matter in the Time Traveler's exact words, we should have shown *him* far less skepticism, because although Filby was obviously full of shit, H.G.'s Richmond neighbor was still more believable than the Time Traveler.

For most certainly, our general evaluation was that we should have easily perceived Filby's motives: a pork-butcher could understand Filby without ever punching the dimwit in the chops with his handy pork or lamb chop. But the Time Traveler had more than a touch of whim among his unique behavioral elements, and we often distrusted his "chicanery", often believing that our cavalier storytelling friend was an absolute charlatan.

Even the gullible people who took H.G. Wells seriously never felt quite sure of his peculiar deportment; most of his acquaintances were somehow aware that trusting their reputations for having association with him was like furnishing a nursery school with eggshell china along with a variety of licentious sex toys. So, I don't think any of us who had attended the bizarre dinner that Thursday evening said very much about time traveling in the weekly interval between that night and the next Thursday supper, although his theory's odd potentialities ran, no doubt, deeply inside most of our miniscule minds: the model Time Machine's implausible disappearance, that is to say, its practical incredibleness, which included the curious possible applications of usable anachronism, not to mention the utter confusion that accompanied the T.T.'s bullshit, had together strongly suggested to us the possibility of a cute canard being enacted.

For my own part, I was particularly preoccupied with the trick of the vanishing model. I remembered discussing with the Medical Man, whom I had met on Friday at the popular Linaean City Bordello, where we were both getting full body massages from a pair of high-priced hookers. The blowhard physician related to me that he had seen a similar thing at the Tübingen Metropolitan Brothel, and laid considerable stress upon the blowing-out of the candles, as his hooker was blowing-out his excess semen from his erect dingle. But exactly how the magic trick was done, the self-important Doctor could not explain, as the portly fool excitedly was preoccupied reaching the climax of his faulty explanation.

The next Thursday evening, I again curiously took a cab to Richmond to honor *our* weekly dinner appointment. I suppose I was one of the Time Traveler's most constant guest, and arriving late, found four or five men already-assembled inside his comfortable drawing-room, which to my knowledge, never artistically drew anything of significance or consequence. The Medical Man was impatiently standing before the fire with a sheet of paper in one hand and his gold fob watch and chain in the other. I looked around the chamber for the Time Traveler. "It's already half-past seven now," impetuously complained the famished Medical Man. "I suppose we'd better start dinner without our host Wells, who I suspect knows volumes about drilling for water and oil!"

"Where's Herbert George?" I asked, naming our absent host.

"You've just come into the room?" the Psychologist asked. "It's rather odd, indeed. Obviously, our friend, frugal Wells, is unavoidably detained, probably buying used condoms at the neighborhood Goodwill Store. He asks me in this note to lead-off with dinner at seven if he's not back from doing some official business. Says he'll explain everything when he eventually arrives."

"It seems a pity to let the dinner spoil," said the hungry Editor of the well-known daily paper; and thereupon, the impulsive Doctor rang the bell for Mrs. Watchett, who liked to habitually eavesdrop on our weekly conversations and curiously witness everything that transpired.

The cynical Psychologist, the skeptical Medical Doctor, and critical Blank, the empty-headed newspaper editor, all had attended the previous Thursday night dinner. The other two guests were a certain young journalist, and a quiet, shy man with a beard, whom I didn't know, and who, as far as my observation went, never opened his mouth all the evening, so I immediately suspected that the new invitee had been suffering from a serious case of lockjaw.

There was some speculation at the dinner-table about the Time Traveler's strange and unusual absence, and I suggested in a half-joking spirit that our dilatory host had been actively time-traveling, probably visiting futuristic whorehouses. The two new arrivals wanted *that* subject explained to them, and the Psychologist volunteered a wooden account of the "ingenious paradox and trick" we had astonishingly witnessed the Thursday before. The Freudian Fraud was in the midst of his monotonous dissertation when the door from the corridor opened, slowly and without any creaking noise. I was facing the portal, and was the first to notice the disheveled-in-appearance Time Traveler. "Hallo!" I yelled. "At last; you've arrived!"

And then, the door opened wider, and the unkempt-looking Time Traveler stood before us in what appeared to be a disoriented state of mind. I gave a shriek of utter surprise and alarm.

"Good heavens, man! What the hell's the matter?" cried the Medical Man, who saw him next. And the whole tableful of astounded diners instantly turned towards the open door.

Our perplexed host was in an amazing plight. Wells' coat was dusty and dirty, and smeared with green slime down the sleeves; his hair quite disordered, and as it seemed to me, much greyer, and in complete disarray. Either his scalp was corroded with grime and dirt, or perhaps the color of his hair had actually faded. H.G.'s face was ghastly pale; his chin had a wide brown cut upon it, featuring a scar that was half-healed; his expression was both haggard and drawn, as if caused by intense suffering. For a moment, the Time Traveler hesitated inside the open doorway, as if he had been dazzled by the room's bright light.

Then Herbert George came forward into the dining area as if he had a six-pound fecal load in his underwear. The extraordinary fellow walked with just such a limp as I have seen exhibited by footsore tramps. Everyone seated around the oval table stared in amazed silence at the battered-looking inventor, expecting him to speak.

The 'T.T.' said not a word, but slowly trudged painfully to the table, and made a motion towards the wine. The Editor filled a glass of sparkling champagne, and nervously pushed the object towards the new arrival. Wells voraciously drained the liquid in three huge gulps, and it seemed to do him good as some color appeared upon his cheeks: for his pupils looked around the table, and the ghost of his old smile slowly flickered across his face.

"What on earth have you been up to, man?" curiously inquired the Doctor. The Time Traveler did not seem to hear the physician's entreaty.

"Don't let me disturb your appetizers," H.G. stated, with a certain faltering articulation. "I didn't have a second circumcision done, so

I'm not petered-out, and am all right. I've just an hour-or-so ago been rather involved in a little futuristic pugilism!"

The Time Traveler stopped his oddball rhetoric, held out his glass for more champagne, and swallowed the substance-down at a draught. "That's mighty good," he appreciatively declared. His eyes suddenly grew brighter, and a faint florid color became more obvious onto his cheeks. H.G.'s glance flickered over to our concerned faces with a certain dull approval, and then our host ambled around the warm room seven times, as if participating in a weirdo roller derby without any skates upon his feet.

Then, the renowned experimenter spoke again, still as if he was awkwardly feeling his way among his words. "I'm going to go upstairs and immediately wash, dress, and take care of this smelly huge dump in my pants and undergarments, and soon I'll come-down and explain things as thoroughly as I can. Save me some of that delicious mutton. To hell with this current vegetarian bullshit vogue! I'm starving for a bit of honest-to-goodness meat."

The Time Traveler looked across at the always-skeptical Editor, who was a rare visitor eating medium-rare mutton, and hoped our host was mentally all right. The puzzled Editor began enunciating a question, which was instantly interrupted by our grimy-looking host. "I'll tell you my adventure presently," announced the Time Traveler. "I'm funny! But I have no intention of performing stand-up at the local comedy club! I'll be all right in a London minute or so. I simply need to adapt my five senses to this once familiar, non-threatening environment!"

The unpredictable Time Traveler put-down his twice-emptied glass, and clumsily paced towards the adjacent staircase. Again, I remarked to the other seated guests his lameness and the soft-padding sound of his footfall, and then standing-up in my place, I observed his feet as H.G. exited, staggering out of the dining room. Wells had nothing upon his walking arrangements except a pair of tattered, blood-stained socks. Then, the door closed upon him.

I had half a mind to follow his path upstairs, until I remembered how our host detested any fuss or bother about himself, or about his ordinary abnormal deportment. For a minute, perhaps, my mind was wool-gathering, as I foolishly contemplated wrestling in a major tournament with harmless sheep. "Remarkable Queer Behavior of an Eminent Scientist," I then heard the Editor articulate his lackluster stereotype, thinking (after his wont) in terms of third-grade catchy newspaper headlines. And *that* mundane commentary brought my attention back to the bright dinner-table.

"What's the game?" said the rather-appalled neophyte Journalist. "Has he been doing the Amateur Old Codger Cadger? I don't follow his peculiar deportment. Mr. Wells must need some female muffins to munch on."

My pupils met the brown eyes of the Psychologist, who perceptively read my own interpretation as evident in his facial expression. I thought of the Time Traveler limping painfully upstairs. I don't think anyone else had observed his involuntary lameness.

The first to recover completely from this fantastic surprise was the Medical Man, who rang the dinner-bell to appease his gargantuan appetite. The equally-famished Editor turned to his knife and fork with a grunt, and the bearded Silent Man followed suit. The dinner was resumed. Conversation was exclamatory for a little while, with gaps of wonderment being visually exchanged; and then the Editor got fervent in divulging his curiosity.

"Does our friend eke out his modest income with studying and pursuing a drama acting career? Or does he have his Nebuchadnezzar or Nostradamus moments?" the newspaper bureaucrat humorously asked.

"I feel assured that his strange behavior involves this nebulous business of the Time Machine," I answered, and took-up the Psychologist's account of our previous meeting. The new guests were frankly incredulous by my serious rendition of past events. The Editor raised several salient objections.

"What *is* this time traveling nonsense? Someone, please explain the soap opera fiction to me in detail. A man couldn't cover himself with dust by theatrically rolling in a damned paradox, could he?" And then, as the idea came home to him, the Editor traveled from the front page to the comic section of his newspaper as he resorted to describing a caricature. "What dumb-ass drama is being enacted? Don't the irresponsible residents of the future have any clothes-brushes or combs?"

The young Journalist too, would not believe the Time Traveler's dusty appearance at any price, and joined the Editor in the easy work of heaping additional ridicule upon the whole sequence of fucked-up events. The mediocre pair were both fickle products of the new breed of journalists; very joyous, irreverent, and hyper-suspicious 'headlines' men'. "I'll wager that Our Special Correspondent in the Day after Tomorrow will inform us on the maladies and sudden decline of civilization," the presumptuous Reporter was ranting and shouting, just as the incredible Time Traveler came back into the room. Mr. Wells was dressed in ordinary evening clothes, and nothing save his haggard look remained of the change that had originally startled me.

"I say," the jovial Editor hilariously commented. "These chapped-lipped chaps here say you've been traveling into the middle of next week! Tell us all about the future, will you? Did London Bridge finally fall down? Did Big Ben turn gay, and is now Big Benny?"

The peeved Time Traveler came to the place reserved for him without uttering a single or married word. Wells casually smiled quietly, in his old non-threatening manner. "Listen you muttonheads! Where's my mutton?" H.G. demanded knowing. "What a treat it will be to stick a fork into delectable meat again! I crave mutton!"

"Story!" cried the Editor. "I'm in the newspaper business, and I want to hear a story. Frankly, I believe that it'll be more fictional than factual!"

"Story be damned!" sternly answered the Time Traveler. "I want something substantial to eat. I won't say a word until I get some peptone into my arteries. Thanks. And pass the salt, and please stop peppering me with so many irrelevant questions!"

"One word," said I. "Have you been time traveling?"

"Yes," said the Time Traveler, with his mouth full, nodding his head. "I'll tell you all about it once I've gotten over my painful indigestion and stomach cramps."

"I'd give a shilling a line for a verbatim script," said the Editor. The Time Traveler pushed his glass towards the Silent Man and pinged it with his fingernail; at which the Silent Man, who had been staring at *his* face, started convulsively shaking his arms and hands in a paranoid manner, and poured Wells more potent wine. The rest of the dinner experience was rather uncomfortable. For my own part, sudden questions kept on rising to my lips, and I dared not utter them, as was the same type of restraint demonstrated by the other curious diners. The Journalist tried to relieve the tension by telling anecdotes of Hettie Potter, a prostitute who had died when a spring in her mattress popped-up and shot her ass out of an open third story window.

The Time Traveler devoted his attention to his dinner, and displayed the appetite of a starving tramp. The Medical Man smoked a sagging foot-long cigarette, and intently watched the Time Traveler through his false feminine eyelashes. The Silent Man seemed even more clumsy than usual, and drank champagne with regularity and determination, mostly out of sheer nervousness; apparently trying to control his noticeable bout with Parkinson's.

At last, the Time Traveler pushed his plate away, and looked around the table at us. "I suppose I must apologize," he prefaced. "I was simply starving. I want you chronic gossipers to fully comprehend that I've had a most amazing time." Wells next reached-out his hand for a cigar, and cut-off the end. "But come into the smoking-room; however, don't worry, gentlemen; the smoking-room is not on fire! It's too long a story to tell over greasy plates." And ringing the bell in passing for the servants to empty-off and clean the table, H.G. led the way into the adjoining room.

"You have told Dash, and Mr. Chose about the machine?" he said to me, leaning back in his easy-chair and specifically naming the two new guests.

"But the thing's a mere paradox," interrupted the neurotic Editor. "Your reputation for being deceptive has preceded you!"

"I can't argue with you tonight. I don't mind telling you the whole story, but I won't argue with obsessive, asshole pessimists. I will," Wells went on, "tell you the story of what has happened to me, if you like, but you must refrain from any obnoxious interruptions. I want to tell it. Badly. Most of it will sound like chronic fibbing and lying. So be it! It's true; every damned word of it, all the same. I was in my laboratory at four o'clock, and since then, in *your* four hours, I've lived eight insane days, such days as no human being has ever lived before! I'm nearly worn-out, totally fatigued from utter exhaustion! But I shall not sleep until I've revealed this whole adventure, or should I say 'misadventure' to you. Then, I shall go to bed with my life-size female sex-doll, and perhaps sleep non-stop for forty-eight hours. But no interruptions! Is it agreed?"

"Agreed!" exclaimed the Editor, and the rest of us automatically echoed, "Agreed." And with that brief conversational interaction, the Time Traveler commenced with his dynamic story as I have set it forth. H. G. at first sat back in his leather chair, and spoke like a weary man lying upon his deathbed. Afterwards, his movements (none from his bowels) became more animated.

In recalling and presently writing-down his unbelievable account, I feel, with only too much keenness, the inadequacy of pen and ink to reproduce his fantastic narrative. And, above all, I must admit, my own inadequacy in expressing the quality of his ethereal nomenclature positively annoys me.

When you read my knowledgeable summary, I will suppose, you'll comprehend my words attentively enough; but you cannot see the speaker's pallid features; you can't observe his sincere face in the bright circle of the little table lamp, nor can you hear the intonation of his excellent baritone voice. And naturally, you cannot know how his facial expressions followed the twists and turns of his seemingly mythological story!

Most of us dumb-shit listeners were enveloped in shadow during Mr. Wells' lengthy presentation, for the candles in the smoking-room had not been lighted, and only the face of the young Journalist, and the hairy legs of the quivering Silent Man, from the knees downward, were partially illuminated. At first, we all glanced now and again at each other. After a time, the aggregate of listeners ceased doing our occasional random glimpses, and the speaker's intrigued audience looked only at the Time Traveler's determined face.

Chapter 3

"TIME TRAVELING"

"I have contended with *your* abundant criticisms, especially from my Editor, from my' Psychologist, and from my' Medical Doctor friend, but despite your academic preparations and knowledge that you have achieved in your very profitable professions, actually, what you accomplish daily, in the final analysis, is quite ephemeral and meaningless. A mere hundred years from now, no one will know or care how many editorials you had written, or how many minds you had salvaged, or precisely how many bodies you have cured!" the Time Traveler defensively maintained and chastised.

"Are you mocking our occupations and our individual dignities?" the Medical Doctor vehemently challenged. "I believe that I, along with your other dinner guests, am being insulted by both your unwarranted allegations and by your malicious insinuations!"

"Yes, Doctor. I *am* deliberately diminishing your professional contribution to society, as well as those achievements of my other dinner visitors," the Time Traveler scoffed. "For you see, a century from now, universities and scientists will be heralding the Time Machine that I have invented, and my marvelous invention will indeed change all aspects of civilized life. Do not compare what you do for a living to how my amazing device will revolutionize both civilization and technology for the better!"

"Go ahead with your fanciful story, but after condemning your friends' distinguished careers," the Editor defiantly stated as the Psychologist and the Doctor nodded their heads in full agreement, "your fucked-up fictional recollections better not give us indigestion and diarrhea!"

"You perverted 'gentlemen', and I use the term loosely," the Time Traveler emphasized, "are exclusively biological beings who

29

think mostly about sex, porno magazines, gluttony, and money! In order to be a dedicated inventor and experimenter, one must be chaste and pure of mind, a sort of Sir Galahad in quest of the Holy Grail. The only thing that really matters to the true scientist is discovery, and not the regular fortune and fame that accompany it!"

"I'm mortified by your inflammatory remarks!" the flabbergasted Editor replied. "I feel inclined to rise from my chair and leave!"

"I'm humiliated and equally offended!" confirmed the Psychologist. "I think that you, Mr. Wells, envy my great fortune and reputation!"

"I'm also chagrined by your verbal harassment," the embarrassed Medical Doctor chimed-in. "But I'll stay and listen to your latest dramatic fiction."

"Fiction is closely related to science, just as hypothesis is connected to the art of imagination," the Time Travel shrewdly answered. "Non-fiction writing, as is evidenced by newspaper journalism, for example, is easy to write, because it's based on mere description or opinion. Fiction writing and science both deal with higher-level thinking skills, such as creativity and self-actualization!"

"Enough of your philosophical bullshit!" the Newspaper Editor orally concluded. "Commence with your story, and if it has validity and merit, and is believable, I'll then acknowledge its veracity!"

"All right, my doubting guests. Here is my testimony about my time travel adventure into the distant future!" Wells sanctimoniously replied. "I had told several of you absurd cynics last Thursday of the general principles of the Time Machine, and demonstrated to you miserable students of Diogenes the actual mechanism itself, incomplete in my workshop, which is actually my *labor*atory, where I assiduously labor. There it is now, the actual, authentic, full-scale model, a little travel-worn, truly; and one of the ivory bars is a trifle cracked, and a brass rail on the right slightly bent; but the rest of the full-size mechanism is sound enough. I had expected to finish manufacturing the time-transportation device on Friday; but on Friday, when the putting together was nearly done, I found that one of the nickel bars was exactly one inch too short, and this I had to get remade; so that the fully-functional Time Machine was not complete until early this morning."

"It was just this afternoon that the first of all Time Machines began its historic career. I gave it a last tap, tightened all the screws again, put one more drop of oil upon the vital quartz rod, and sat myself inside the saddle which was designed after the American Old West cowboy horse riders' seat. I suppose a suicide who holds a pistol to his skull feels much the same wonder at what will come next as my vacillating emotions had felt then. I firmly grabbed the starting lever in one hand, and the stopping one in the other, pressed the first grip, and almost immediately audaciously pushed in the second. I seemed to reel and gyrate as if being involved in a sudden earthquake; I felt a nightmare sensation of falling; and, looking round, I saw the laboratory exactly as before. Had anything happened? For a moment, I suspected that my in-a-quandary intellect, and my dubious eyes, had tricked me. Then, I noticed the wall clock. A moment before, as it seemed, it had stood at a minute or so past the hour; now the instrument read nearly half-past!"

"I drew a breath, set my teeth, gripped the aforementioned starting lever with both hands, and zoomed-off with a definite thud. The laboratory became hazy, vague, and soon transitioned into partial darkness. Mrs. Watchett entered the laboratory, and obliviously walked around, apparently without observing me whirling and swirling about; her destination was apparently towards the garden door. I suppose it took my' dependable housekeeper a minute or so to traverse the distance, but to me she seemed to shoot across the room like a damned misguided rocket. Gaining courage, I pressed the lever over to its extreme position. The night came like the turning-out of a lamp, and in another moment came tomorrow. The laboratory environment grew faint and hazy; then fainter and ever fainter. Tomorrow night came black, then day again, night again, day again, faster and faster still. An eddying murmur filled my ears, and a strange, dumb confusion descended upon my mind. I thought that my senses were entering a fucked-up phase of insanity!"

"I am afraid, gentlemen, that I cannot convey the peculiar sensations associated with time traveling, which are exceedingly unpleasant, nauseous and distasteful. There is a feeling exactly like one has upon a switchback roller coaster, of a sickening sensation; a helpless headlong motion! I was on the verge of regurgitating my early morning breakfast. I felt the same horrible anticipation, too, of an imminent smash. Time traveling was similar to being on a merry-go-round, but the platform is going twelve times its normal rotation speed, and the track that the carousel horse you're riding upon is warped, so the rider has a rapidly-occurring circular path, along with an extremely terrible up-and-down experience, all happening simultaneously!"

"As I picked-up pace, night followed day like the flapping of a crow's black wing. The dim suggestion of the laboratory seemed presently to fade-away from my visual perception, and I curiously observed the sun hopping swiftly across the sky, leaping and bounding every minute, and every minute, I ascertained, marking a day. I supposed that the laboratory had then been destroyed or disintegrated, and my machine and I had entered into the open air. My eyes had a dim impression of rising and falling scaffolding, but I was already going too fast to be conscious of any friggin' moving things. The slowest snail that ever crawled dashed by too fast for me to even identify."

"The twinkling succession of darkness and light was excessively painful and straining to my pupils. Then, in the intermittent darkness, I saw the nocturnal moon spinning swiftly through its quarters from new to full, and had a faint glimpse of the circling stars, finally comprehending my swift time-speed being in terms of months. Presently, as I zipped on, still gaining velocity, with the mercurial palpitation of night and day merging into one continuous greyness; the sky took on a wonderful deepness going from azure to navy blue, and represented as a splendid, luminous color like that of early twilight, both dawn and dusk; the fluctuating sun became a streak of fire, displaying itself as a brilliant arch, suspended in space; the moon shone as a fainter pulsating band; and instantaneously, I could see nothing of the revolving stars, save now and then a brighter circle glimmering in the distant blue."

"The freakin' landscape was misty and vague. I was still on the current hillside upon which this house had been erected, and the knoll's shoulder rose above me, appearing grey and dim. I saw peculiar-looking trees growing and changing like orchestrated puffs of vapor, now brown, then green, then brown in alternating fashion; the arbors grew, spread, shivered, and ultimately passed-away. My eyes comprehended huge buildings rising-up faint and fair, and predictably passing into infinity like hollow dreams. The whole surface of the Earth seemed changed, melting, shriveling, and flowing like out-of-control floods under my eyes. The indicator hands upon the dials that registered my speed raced around and around, rotating faster and faster. Presently, I noted that the sun belt was swaying-up and down, oscillating from solstice to solstice, in a minute or less, and that consequently my incredible pace was then over a year a minute; and minute-by-minute my pupils perceived white snow flashing across the world's surface, and in split-seconds, the frightening phenomenon vanished, and was soon followed by the bright, brief green of spring."

"The unpleasant sensations of the start were less poignant now as my brain became accustomed to the weird passing time intervals, which, in retrospect, were very extraordinary. The spectacular images merged at last into a kind of hysterical, animated exhilaration. Indeed, the entire event was a clumsy swaying of the machine, for which I was unable to account, or accurately evaluate. But my mind was too addled to attend to interpreting everything I was attempting to assess, so with a kind of madness growing upon me, I intrepidly flung myself further into the future."

"At first, I scarcely thought of abruptly halting; scarce thought of anything but adapting to these new vibrating sensations. But presently, a fresh series of impressions dominated my mind; a certain curiosity, and therewith, accompanied by a certain dread, until at last, their symbiosis took complete possession of my captive mind. 'What strange developments of humanity, what wonderful advances upon our rudimentary civilization might I discover?' I thought; might not appear when I came to look nearly into the dim elusive world that radically raced and danced before my eyes! I viewed great and splendid architecture rising about me, more massive than any famous, tall edifices of our own time, and yet, as it seemed, those fantastic structures seemed constructed of glimmer and mist. I fathomed a richer green flow majestically spreading up the hillside, and the verdant cover remained there, without exhibiting any recurrent wintry intermission. Even through the veil of my total confusion, the Earth seemed very fair, and also, permanent and unchanging. And so, my mind came round to the business of stopping, hoping that the atmosphere had retained sufficient oxygen for my lungs to breathe."

"The peculiar risk that I feared most lay in the possibility of my finding some substance or material in the same space which I, or the machine, would occupy upon stopping. 'No two objects, me included, could occupy the same fuckin' space!' I remember conjecturing. "As long as I had traveled at a high velocity through time, *that* particular consideration scarcely mattered: I was, so to speak, attenuated, and was slipping like a thin vapor through the atoms of intervening substances! But to come to a sudden halt involved the jamming of myself, molecule by molecule, into whatever forms that might lay in my way; my stopping meant bringing my atoms into such intimate contact with those of an already-existing unknown obstacle, that perhaps a profound chemical reaction, possibly a far-reaching explosion would result, and as a result, blow myself and my apparatus out of all possible dimensions, blasting me directly into the vast Unknown Fifth Dimension. That distinct possibility had occurred to me again and again while I had been assembling the very intricate Time Machine; but then, I had cheerfully accepted the prospect of death as an unavoidable risk, one of the dangers that an avid inventor has got to take! Now, the apparent risk was inevitable; I no longer acknowledged the peril in the same cheerful light. The fact is that, insensibly, the absolute strangeness of everything, the sickly jarring and swaying of the amazing machine, above all, the feeling of prolonged falling, had absolutely upset my nerves along with disturbing my cerebral discernment. Despite my overwhelming pessimism, with a gust of petulance, I resolved to stop my daring venture into the future. Like an impatient fool, I desperately lugged over the lever, and *incontinently,* without crapping my trousers, the Time Machine went reeling-over, and I was virtually catapulted headlong through the air."

"The sound of a clap of thunder echoed in my ears. My senses may have been stunned for a brief moment. A pitiless hail was hissing all around me, and I was aware that I had been sitting upon soft turf in front of the overturned machine. Everything still seemed grey, but presently, I remarked to myself that the intense confusion inside my ears and head was gone."

"My eyes searched round me to further investigate my new-found, oddball environment. 'What the hell is all this strange shit!' I remember thinking. I was on what seemed to be a little lawn inside a fabulous garden, surrounded by gorgeous rhododendron and hydrangea bushes, and I noticed that their mauve and purple blossoms were dropping to the ground under the beating of the annoying hailstone shower. The rebounding, dancing hail hung in a little cloud above the overturned machine, and the disturbing pattern drove along the ground like a flitting sheet of smoke. In a moment, I was soaking wet to the skin. 'Fine hospitality,' said I, 'to a curious man who has traveled innumerable years to see you. Frankly, though! I'm just glad to still be alive'!"

"Presently gentlemen, I thought what a fool I was to be getting somewhat saturated. I hesitated, and then stood-up and looked around in wonder. Astounded, a colossal figure, evidently carved in some white stone, loomed indistinctly beyond the rhododendrons and hydrangeas through the hazy downpour of hail sheets. But all else of the future world was at that moment indiscernibly indistinct."

"My general visual sensations would be hard to describe. As the columns of hail grew thinner, and the rainstorm diminished, I focused my eyes and saw the overhead white figure more vividly. It was very enormous, for a rather-high silver birch-tree merely touched its left shoulder. The 'monument' was of magnificent white marble, in the general shape of something resembling a winged sphinx, but the wings, instead of being carried vertically at the sides, were spread-out at the shoulders, so that the artificial bird seemed to be hovering. The pedestal, it appeared to me, was constructed of bronze, and was thick with patina. It chanced that the figure's stern face was pointing directly towards me; the sightless eyes seemed to watch my very deliberate movements; and yes, there was the faint shadow of a smirk-type smile upon the marble creature's closed lips."

"The 'White Sphinx' was greatly weather-worn, and that imparted an unpleasant suggestion of disease or corrosion, instantly suggesting a lack of care and maintenance. I stood with my mouth agape looking at the odd spectacle for a brief interval, half a minute, perhaps, or perhaps half an hour, for right then and there, time was existing in a sort of suspended animation. The mammoth stone figure seemed to advance and to recede as the hail drove before it, ever-changing, either denser or thinner. At last, I tore my eyes from the huge object's impressive appearance for a moment, and noticed that the hail curtain had worn threadbare, and that the sky was lightening with the promise of the emerging sun improving my perception."

"I glanced-up again at the crouching white shape, and the full temerity of my voyage came suddenly descending upon my feeling of complete alienation. What might appear when that hazy curtain was altogether withdrawn? What might not have happened to men, and to civilization? What if cruelty had grown into a common passion and had degenerated into despair? What if, in this interval, the human race had lost its desire to advance with new technology and science, and consequently, had developed into something diabolical, unsympathetic, and overwhelmingly powerful? I might seem to the current residents like some old-world savage animal, only the more dreadful and disgusting for *our* common likeness; the inhabitants regarding me as a foul creature to be condemned and slain."

"Already, with the lifting of the haze, I saw other vast shapes in the distance; colossal buildings with intricate parapets, along with tall columns, with a wooded hillside dimly creeping-in upon me through the lessening distant storm, where wonderful Richmond in London once flourished."

"My heart was immediately seized with a panic fear. I turned frantically to the Time Machine, and strove hard to upright it, and methodically readjust its operating gearshifts, if I might require initiating an emergency escape. As I did so, the illuminating shafts of the sun beamed through the vanishing thunderstorm. The grey downpour had been beneficially swept-aside and quickly evaporated like the trailing garments of a two-dimensional ghost. Above me, in the intense blue of the summer sky, some faint brown shreds of clouds whirled into nothingness."

"The great buildings about me stood-out, very clear and distinct, shining like gemstones with the wet impact of the recent thunderstorm, and brilliantly showing their fascinating white shapes by the un-melted heaps of accumulated hailstones piled along their courses. I felt naked in a strange new world. I felt as perhaps an ordinary bird may feel in the clear air, knowing that the predator hawk wings above, and will soon avariciously swoop-down."

"My fear ascended to a burgeoning frenzy. I took a ten-inhalation breathing exercise, set my teeth, and again grappled fiercely, wrist and knee, with righting the heavy Time Machine. It gave under my desperate onset, and finally turned-over to its normal position. However, in my mania, the dashboard violently struck my chin and caused a mild gash below my lips. With one hand upon the western saddle, the other upon the lever, I stood erect, panting heavily with a powerful impulse to mount again."

"But with this seemingly triumphant recovery, I boldly forget about implementing a prompt retreat, as my courage soon recovered. I looked more curiously, and less fearfully, at this world of the remote future. In a circular opening, high-up in the wall of the nearer house, I noticed a group of short figures, all clad in rich soft robes.

The residents had seen my struggling behaviors, and their faces were directed towards my location."

"Then, my ears heard weird voices, sounding like those of fucked-up ventriloquists, approaching from the east. Coming through the bushes by the White Sphinx were the heads and shoulders of little individuals, all running in my direction. One of these emerged in a pathway leading straight to the little lawn upon which I stood with my very special machine, which was my only means of escape from this newly-discovered, extraordinary setting. The miniature fellow was a slight, weak-looking creature, perhaps four-feet-tall, and was clad in a purple tunic, girdled at the waist with a leather belt. Sandals or buskins, I could not clearly distinguish which, were worn upon his tiny feet; his legs were bare to the knees, and his partially-bald head was also nearly bald. Understanding *that* rather surreal scenario, I noticed for the first time how warm the air actually was."

"This 'midget-man' struck me as being a very beautiful and graceful creature, but indescribably frail and non-threatening. His flushed face reminded me of the more beautiful kind of medieval suavity associated with past regal royalty as represented in museum portraits; yes, an ideal cherub image; that hectic beauty of which we used to hear and read so much about in encyclopedias. At the sight of him, I suddenly regained my self-confidence. I took my hands from the machine and desired to establish some imaginative form of genuine conversation. Did these 'beautiful people' engage in mental telepathy as opposed to verbal speech? Will my voice harshly hurt their auditory perception? Should I use hand gestures in attempting to explain my primitive ideas? At that particular moment, I felt more at ease, so obviously, either oral or symbolic communication, I believed, should somehow be cordially initiated."

Chapter 4

"IN THE GOLDEN AGE"

"In another moment, we were standing face-to-face, I, looking-down, and this fragile, pint-sized specimen out of the future peering upwards. He, apparently a male, or perhaps a transgender, had come straight-up to me and incessantly laughed directly into my eyes. The absence of him bearing any sign of fear or anxiety struck me at once as being rather infantile and abnormal. Then, the futuristic Lilliputian turned to the two other comrades of his species, whom to my recognition, were like zombie disciples following his lead, and the head fellow softly spoke to his apostles in a strange, very sweet and fucked-up, liquid tongue."

"There were other dwarfish individuals scurrying through the high shrubbery, and presently, a little group of perhaps eight or ten of those exquisite creatures were chattering nonsense, and soon examining my presence from twenty-feet-away. One of them endeavored addressing me in what sounded like a toddler's foreign language; indeed, rather disorganized gibberish. It came into my head, oddly enough, that my voice was too harsh and deep for their supersensitive ears. So, I methodically shook my head, and, pointing to my ears, shook it again, trying to diligently communicate the elementary thought that they and I should listen, for the expressed purpose of establishing some form of basic communication. Amazingly, hardly any reaction occurred among my short-attention-span companions."

"The seemingly adolescent, blond-haired midget approached a step forward, hesitated, and then, as would a curious toddler, reached-forward and touched my hand. Then, I felt other soft little tentacles feeling upon my back and shoulders. Those asshole fools wanted to make sure that I was real, and not some kind of extraordinary three-dimensional mirage. There was nothing in that odd encounter that was at all particularly alarming or threatening. Indeed, there was something in these pretty little people that inspired a subtle confidence, a graceful gentleness, in addition to a certain childlike ease. I decided that I should gradually pursue my academic inquiry to the next level."

"And besides my initial perception, those miniature humans looked so frail and wimpy that I, without being a bowling ball, could fancy myself flinging the whole dozen-and-a-half of the stupid-shits about like ninepins if I suddenly needed to defend myself. But I made a swift motion with my right hand to warn the entourage when I noticed several of their little pink hands (including their tiny pinkies) curiously feeling at the Time Machine's dashboard."

"Happily, then, when it was not too late, I thought of an immediate danger that I had hitherto forgotten, and reaching over the bars of the recently successful teleportation mechanism, I gingerly unscrewed the little levers that would set my time transportation vehicle into motion, and I carefully put those small objects inside my pants' pocket. With *that* necessity being easily and urgently accomplished, matters again seemed to be copesetic, so I turned again toward my short, new, weirdo chums to see what I could do in regard to resuming some rudimentary exchange of words."

"And then, looking more nearly into their simplistic, nondescript features, I observed some further peculiarities in their Dresden-China-type of kindergarten prettiness. Their blond hair, which was uniformly curly, came to a sharp end at the neck and cheek. Also, there was not the faintest suggestion of whiskers, beards, or mustaches on what I assumed were male faces, and furthermore, their ears were singularly minute-in-size, and quite pointed. Their mouths were small, with bright red, rather-thin lips, and their little chins beneath their dumb-ass grins were tapered to a central point. The beady eyes of those apparent morons were larger than ordinary, and quite shrunken in appearance; and this may seem like some ethnocentric egotism on my part, but I sensed and fancied that there was a certain lack of the intellectual interest and subsequent fascination I might have expected in their stupid-shit deportment."

"The group seemed to lack a definitive leader or spokesman. As no one in the oddball bevy made any gesture, or intentional effort, to communicate with me, but simply stood around my erect form smiling and speaking in soft cooing notes to each other, I began what constituted a ridiculous conversation to learn more of their seemingly mediocre culture. I pointed my index finger first to the Time Machine, and next to myself. Then, hesitating for a moment on how I should express the abstract concept of 'Time', I symbolically pointed to the bright sun. At once, a quaint, pretty little asshole, garbed in checkered purple and white, followed my gesticulation, and then the diminutive dolt astonished me by bizarrely imitating a loud clasp of thunder."

"For a moment, I was genuinely staggered, although the import of his gesture was plain enough to be astutely interpreted. The question had come into my mind rather abruptly: were these' fucked-up, miniature creatures imbecilic fools who sleep in cribs and cavort-around in playpens? You may hardly understand how their frivolous mannerisms had affected me. You see, I had always anticipated that the people of the year Eight Hundred and Two Thousand odd would be incredibly in front of us primitive Victorians in knowledge, in art, well, in everything."

"Then, one of the future lame-brained natives suddenly asked me a remote question that showed him to be on the intellectual level of one of our five-year-old nursery school children; asked me, in fact, if I had come from the sun in a local thunderstorm! It let loose confirmation of the suspicious judgment which I had rendered upon their uniformed clothes, upon their frail, lily-white, flaccid limbs, and upon their fragile features. A flow of negative disappointment stampeded across my disenchanted mind. For a moment, I felt that I had built the Time Machine in vain."

"I was both anticipating and expecting to confront futuristic versions of British Sir Isaac Newton, of the Italian Leonardo da Vinci, or of the American inventive genius, Thomas Edison, who, in regard to hours and minutes, kept all of the clocks in his Menlo Park, New Jersey laboratory at the wrong times so that his employees would be unconcerned with the exact time of day. Most certainly, Michelangelo, Socrates, Plato, Aristotle and Galileo facsimiles these miniature nincompoops were not!"

"I nodded to indicate my compatibility with the illiterate dunce's two-word sentences, pointed to the sun, and gave the little assholes such a vivid rendering of a thunderclap that the loud impact of my hands seemingly startled the living feces out of their farting assholes. The pack of tiny idiots all withdrew a pace or so, and together bowed their heads in either surrender or submission. Truthfully, I felt compelled and motivated to spank and beat the shit and piss out of the entire fucked-up ensemble."

"Then, one little blond-hair knucklehead came laughing towards me, carrying a chain of beautiful flowers, which were altogether new to my' botanical knowledge, and the bizarre birdbrain placed the delicate necklace around my bowed neck. The benevolent act was received with melodious applause and silly clapping from his fickle associates; and presently thereafter, the entire contingent of stupid-shits were all scampering-around, dashing to-and-fro in order to pick more colorful flowers, and next, laughingly flinging the various petals and blossoms upon me until I was almost completely smothered with picked blooms. And honestly, I had to restrain and discipline myself from physically assassinating the whole bunch of giddy, fatuous fools!"

"I then organized a specific notion inside my abnormally confused brain. 'These ludicrous scamps make my conceited friends, the newspaper Editor, the Medical Doctor, and the psycho Psychologist seem like mental giants,' I theorized and determined. 'At best, these dumb-fuck midgets are ignoramuses!' I instinctively ascertained. 'If I could transport the entire group back to good old 1899, I could make a small fortune sponsoring them in a circus or lucrative stage act! What a terrific way to turn into a new century'!"

"You who have never seen the likes of these small dunderheads can scarcely imagine what delicate and wonderful flowers countless years of agriculture and nature had wondrously created. Then, someone among the ass-backwards clan suggested that their plaything, namely me, should be exhibited inside the nearest building, and so I was led past the classic sphinx of white marble, which had seemed to watch me all the while with a peculiar smile aimed at my gross astonishment, and *we* meandered through a small-woods towards a vast grey edifice composed mostly of fretted stone."

"As I ambled onward with those blond-haired absolute morons, the memory of my confident anticipation of a profoundly advanced and intellectual posterity reentered by muddled mind, which in retrospect, occasionally represented irresistible amusement. Soon, the wee folk and I reached *their* intended destination."

"The aforementioned building had a very huge entry, and its interior was of colossal dimensions. My mind was naturally most preoccupied with the growing crowd of little people, and also with the big open portals that yawned before my presence, both massive panels being shadowy and rather-mysterious. My general impression of the world my eyes beheld while glancing over their heads on our abbreviated trek to the large structure was a tangled waste of beautiful bushes and flowers, and the open-air entrance was encompassed by a long-neglected, and yet, weedless garden."

"Along the irregular and meandering forest path, I had observed a number of tall-spiked white flowers, the exceptional arrangements measuring perhaps a foot across the spread of the alluring waxen petals. The colorful array grew scattered, as if wild, among the variegated shrubs. But, as I say, being distracted, I did not examine the myriad kinds of vegetation very closely at that particular time. I recollected that the Time Machine had been left deserted upon the turf, facing the White Sphinx, nestled among the various rhododendron and hydrangea bushes, so I was confident that the mechanism could not be accidentally activated by one of these foolish cultural retards."

"The arch of the entrance doorway to the immense building to which I had been escorted was richly carved, but naturally, I did not observe the artistic design very thoroughly, although my mind fancied that I had observed impressions of old Phoenician and

Egyptian decorations as I hurriedly passed through. And it struck me that the overall foreign wall ornaments were very badly broken and weather-worn. Several more brightly clad people met me inside the vast doorway, and so we entered together; I, dressed in dingy nineteenth-century garments, looking grotesque enough, but still garlanded with alien flowers, and surrounded by an eddying mass of bright, soft-colored robes and shining white body limbs. The clan members' vocal cords engaged in a melodious whirl of asinine laughter, combined with silly speech patterns."

"The enormous doorway gave way into a proportionately great hall hung with dull, faded, brown drapes. The beige ceiling was in dark shadow, and the chamber's windows, partially glazed with colored glass, and others partially unglazed, admitted a tempered light inside what appeared to be a cafeteria setting. The floor was composed of huge blocks of some very hard white metal, not plates or slabs, but of solid granite blocks, and it was so much worn and in need of replacement, as I judged by the going to-and-fro of countless past generations, as to be so irregularly channeled along the more frequented borders."

"Throughout the length and breadth of the in-shambles edifice, innumerable tables had been fabricated of polished stone, raised, perhaps, a foot from the floor, and upon these were heaps of fruits arranged inside of large, red bowls. Some of the exotic food I recognized as a kind of hypertrophied raspberry, and also a tropical variety of orange, but for the most part, the edibles were strange and foreign to my knowledge or my vocabulary. However, I continued to visually investigate my surroundings."

"Between the tables were scattered a great number of comfortable cushions. Upon these my conductors and guides seated themselves, signing for me to do likewise in simulated Japanese fashion. With a pretty absence of ceremony, or any semblance of religious prayer, the indigenous numbskulls began consuming the attractive fruit with their hands, flinging peel and stalks, and so forth, into the round wide openings in the sides of the tables. No evidence of any forks, knives, plates, napkins or spoons had been placed upon the circular tables. I soon followed their rather impetuous example, for I felt both thirsty and hungry from surviving my grueling time voyage. As I did so, and partook of my fruit meal, I casually surveyed the great hall at my leisure. The entire place was in need of total maintenance."

"And perhaps the thing that struck me most was the huge room's dilapidated and unkempt appearance. The stained-glass windows, which displayed only a simple geometrical pattern, were broken in many sections, and the curtains that hung across the lower end of the hall were quite thick with abundant dust accumulation. And it caught my attention that the corner of the marble table near me had been fractured, and not repaired."

"Nevertheless, the general effect of the large cafeteria was extremely rich and picturesque. There were, perhaps, three hundred blond-haired idiots dining inside the hall, and most of the company made sure that they had been seated as near to me as the diners could possibly come, perhaps as a sign of interest, or perhaps out of a need to feel emotionally secure. The little rascals were watching me with keen interest; their beady eyes being occasionally aware of the tasty fruit that they were discourteously grabbing from the red bowls and then bringing to their mouths, and next ravenously swallowing. All of the little bastards were clad in the same soft, and yet resilient, silk-like material."

"Harvested fruit constituted their entire diet. Essentially, these mentally-deficient people of the remote future were strict vegetarians, and while I was in their' absurd company, in spite of some carnal meat cravings, I had to conform to their fruit-oriented diet, also. Indeed, I had soon found afterwards that horses, cattle, sheep, dogs, cats, mice and the like had followed the various dinosaurs into extinction. But needless to say, the available fruits were very delightful in flavor; one, in particular, that seemed to be in season all the time I was there, was a floury delectable, having a three-sided husk; it was especially good and sweet, and I made it my staple."

"At first, I was tremendously puzzled by all of those strange and unidentified fruits, and also by the marvelous flowers that my eyes especially valued, but later I began to objectively perceive *their* mind-boggling import, as I shall explicitly describe in a few moments."

"However, I am telling *you,* my' gregarious Thursday evening dinner friends, of my incredible fruit supper I had been enjoying and savoring in the distant future. So, as soon as my appetite had been satisfied, I determined to make a resolute attempt to learn the speech and basic vocabulary patterns of these new dumb-fuck acquaintances of mine. Clearly, and out of sheer necessity, that was the next viable task to do. The fruits seemed a convenient subject upon which to begin my impromptu seminar, and holding one of those raspberry-type edibles up in front of their pallid faces, I began a series of interrogative sounds and gestures. However, much to my disappointment, I had considerable difficulty in conveying my simple interrogation."

"At first, my futile efforts met with stares of surprise, or of inextinguishable laughter, but presently, a fair-haired little creature seemed to grasp my intention and repeated a rather weird noun. The entire group had to chatter and explain the business at great length to each other, and my first attempts to make the exquisite little sounds of their lackluster language caused an immense amount of genuine, if not uncivil, raucous amusement amongst themselves. However, I felt like a frustrated schoolmaster instructing and eliciting ludicrous terminology amidst attention-deficit children, and I wholeheartedly persisted, and presently, I had a score of noun substantives extracted from their unsophisticated nomenclature, at least at my command; and then, I remarkably got to enunciating the demonstrative pronouns 'This, That, These, and Those', and eventually arrived at the action-verb/infinitive 'to eat'."

"But the entire educational process was very slow, methodical work, and the little people soon tired and wanted to evade participation in my fundamental academic interrogations, so I determined, rather of necessity, to let the little jerk-offs provide their challenging revelations to me in little doses when their under-developed acumens felt so inclined. And very little doses I found the picayune imbeciles were capable of enduring, for I never met people more indolent, or more easily fatigued over attempting to express and communicate actual pre-school, kindergarten-type tasks."

Jay Dubya

Chapter 5

"THE SUNSET OF CIVILIZATION"

" A rather queer insight I soon discovered about my little, lackluster-brained, future hosts, and that was their noticeable lack of interest in anything that required any degree of thought or labor. These lethargic, non-conscientious, non-industrious, basically lazy dumb-shits were indeed, wholly reprehensible, and in essence, virtually contemptible to anyone who values progress. The pathetic dipsticks would come-up to me with eager cries of astonishment, like pouting and sulking children seeking adult approval, but, just like short-attention-span youngsters, the group would soon stop examining me, and then wander-away, seeking some other prospective toy."

"The cafeteria-style dinner, along with my conversational beginnings, had ended, and I noted for the first time that almost all of those empty-headed dimwits who had surrounded me at first were quickly dispersed and soon gone. It is odd, too, how speedily I came to disregard these 'little dolts' with any sort of personal fascination. I went-out through the same front portal into the sunlit world, that is to say, as soon as my hunger had been entirely satisfied. In my stroll, I was continually meeting more of these oddball 'dumb-ass folks of the future', who would follow me a little distance behind my casual saunter; chatter and laugh about me, and, having smiled and gesticulated in a weird-but-friendly way, leave me again to my own interests. To tell the truth, the entire scenario was totally aggravating!"

"The calm of evening was soon upon the world, as I emerged further-away from the great hall. The magnificent scenery was lit by the warm glow of the setting sun. At first, things I observed were very confusing, bouncing around inside my disheveled mind. Every experience was so entirely different from the familiar work-oriented

1899 world I had known, even the sensational flowers and trees I admired."

"The big building which I had left was situated upon the slope of a broad river valley, but the Thames of 1899 had shifted drastically in the future, perhaps a mile west from its present position. I resolved to climb to the summit of a nearby crest, several miles away to the north, from which I could get a wider view of this, our unique planet, in the year Eight Hundred and Two Thousand Seven Hundred and One, A.D. For that, I should adequately explain, was the date that the little dashboard dials of my machine had accurately recorded. All the while, as I clambered higher up the hill, my distressed mind was sorting-out what my disbelieving eyes were witnessing."

"As I walked and wandered-about, I was watching for any impression that could possibly help to explain the general condition of ruinous splendor in which I found the unraveled world, for ruinous, indeed, it was. A little way up the steep hill, for instance, was a great heap of granite, bound together by masses of aluminum; yes, a vast labyrinth of precipitous walls along with crumpled and twisted metal beams, amidst which were thick piles of very beautiful pagoda-like plants, and myriad nettles, but wonderfully tinted with brown markings about the leaves, and seemingly incapable of stinging my skin. The materials' dump was evidently the derelict remains of some former vast structure, but to what purpose that the demolished architecture had been built, I could not assess or determine. It was there that I was destined, at a later date, to have a very strange encounter, which was the first intimation of a still-terribly stranger discovery, but of *that* manifestation, I shall speak and describe in its proper chronological place."

"Looking around the general vicinity, with a sudden speculation, from a terrace upon which I rested for a while, I realized that there were no small houses anywhere to be seen. Apparently, the single-family home, and possibly even the usual household organization, had vanished into non-existence. Here and there among the greenery were enormous palace-like buildings, but the ordinary 1899-style house, bungalow, and traditional cottage, which form such characteristic features of our own British landscape, had incredulously and enigmatically disappeared."

'Communism,' I prematurely evaluated to myself. 'Marxist-Socialism leading to Communism has yielded this pathetic result! The lazy dregs inside a given population lives off of the labors of the wealthy and the industrious, until the rich capitalists run-out of money; become thoroughly disgusted themselves, and then, feeling vanquished, choose to rely on the welfare of the all-tyrannical, controlling government!'

"And on the heels of *that* initial generalization came another disturbing consideration. I looked at the half-dozen little figures that were habitually following me. Then, in a flash realization, I perceived that all had the same form of costume, the same soft hairless visage, and the same girlish rotundity of bodily limbs. It may seem strange, perhaps, that I had not noticed these specific issues before. But everything was so uncanny from the very beginning. Now, I saw the vivid fact plainly enough. In costume, and in all the differences of texture and bearing that now mark off the sexes from each other, these people of the future were alike in physique, almost a fucked-up unisex society. However, among the population, there appeared to be little individuality, or any evidence of unique personalities. And the children seemed to my eyes to be but the mere miniatures of their non-exceptional parents. I judged then that the youngsters of that future time were extremely precocious when compared with their parents, physically at least, and I found afterwards, abundant verification of my original opinion."

"Seeing the ease and security in which these people were living, I felt that this close resemblance of the sexes was, after all, what one would expect once hard labor requiring strength and muscular activity had been eliminated; for the stamina of a man and the softness of a woman, the institution of the family, and the differentiation of occupations are mere militant necessities of an age of physical force."

"Where population is balanced and abundant, much childbearing becomes an evil rather than a blessing to the despotic State; where violence comes but rarely, and offspring are feeling safe and secure, over centuries, there is less necessity, and later on, indeed, there persists no necessity for an efficient family to function, and the specialization of the sexes with reference to their children's needs eventually disappears. Responsibility, as well as male Nature versus female Nurture, loses their meaning. We see some beginnings of *this* evolving phenomenon even in our own time, and in that future age, it had become finalized and complete. This, I must remind you, attentive gentlemen, was my rational thesis at that fragile future time. Later, I was to appreciate how far my erroneous theory fell short of reality."

"While I was mentally musing upon these random, peripheral notions, my attention was attracted by a pretty little structure, like a well situated under an overhead cupola. I thought, in a transitory way, of the oddness of wells still existing in 1899, and then resumed reviewing the thread of my active imagination. There were no large buildings constructed towards the top of the hill, and as my walking powers were evidently beyond the capabilities of the little people following me, I was presently left alone for the first time. With a strange sense of freedom and a quest for adventure, I adamantly ventured-on up to the hill's crest."

"There, I found a seat of some yellow metal that I did not recognize from my former 1899 experience; the material was corroded in places with a kind of pinkish rust, and half-smothered in soft moss; the arm-rests were cast and filed into the resemblance of griffins' heads. I sat-down upon the rubbish pile, and my eyes surveyed the broad view of our 'old world' under the sunset of that long day. It was as sweet and fair a view as I have ever seen."

"The sun's strong glow had already disappeared below the western horizon, and the distant atmosphere was then a flaming gold, touched with some horizontal bars of purple and crimson. Below was the once-familiar valley of the Thames, in which the river lay like a band of burnished steel. I have already spoken of the great massive palaces that dotted about among the variegated greenery, some in ruins, and some still possibly occupied. Here and there rose a white or silvery figure in the waste garden of the Earth, and conversely, here and there came the sharp vertical line of some mysterious cupola or cryptic obelisk. There were no maintained hedges, no signs of proprietary 'no trespassing' rights; no evidence of agricultural activity, nor any indications of factories or industry; the whole earth had become a monotonous, gorgeous, botanical garden."

"So, watching and assessing the overall tranquil environment, I began to put my interpretation upon the distinct observations I had seen, and as it shaped itself to me that evening, my analysis was developing something in this way. But gentlemen; allow me to stress that soon afterwards, I found I had gotten only a half-truth; or as *you* will discover, only a glimpse of one facet of the truth. But I'll not permit my narrative of going too far ahead of itself."

"It seemed to me that I had happened to trespass upon humanity at its wane, descending into de-evolution thousands of years after civilization's halcyon days. The ruddy sunset set me thinking of the declining sunset of mankind. For the first time, I began to realize an odd consequence of the social effort in which we are at present engaged. And yet, come to think of the future social fabric, it is a logical consequence enough. Strength is the outcome of need; security sets a premium on achieving feebleness."

"The work of ameliorating the more challenging and difficult conditions of everyday life, the fruitless effort of government that makes life more and more secure, had gone steadily onward to a disastrous climax. One triumph of a united humanity over Nature had steadily followed another. Accomplishments that are now mere dreams had become projects deliberately put into incompetent hands and carried forward. And the unproductive harvest of eliminating daily work and struggle was what I was then witnessing!"

"After all, the sanitation and the agriculture of today are still in the rudimentary stages of development. The inadequate *science* of our time has successfully attacked but a small aspect of the field of human disease; however, even so, it spreads its operations very steadily and persistently, slowly-but-effectively bleeding-over into the *social sciences* and humanities. Our agriculture and horticulture destroy a weed just here and there, and meagerly cultivate perhaps a score or so of wholesome plants, leaving the greater number to fight out a balance as they can. We almost-miraculously improve our favorite plants and animals through selective breeding; now, a new and better-tasting peach; now, a seedless grape; now, a sweeter and larger flower; and now a more convenient breed of fatted cattle."

"We improve those separate endeavors rather gradually, because our well-intentioned ideals are vague and tentative, and our finite knowledge is very limited; because in our imitation of Mother Nature, too, becomes quite shy and slow in our clumsy, unqualified hands. In short, over eons, our well-intentioned production becomes counterproductive!"

"Someday, all this prolific convolution will be better coordinated, and still better implemented. That is the drift of the mainstream current, in spite of all the abundant, interfering eddies. The whole world's residents will eventually be intelligent, educated, and co-operating; things will move faster and faster towards the complete subjugation of Nature. In the end, wisely and carefully, we shall readjust the balance of animal and vegetable life to suit our human needs. So, gentlemen, I submit to you for your own discernment: is what I have seen in the future justification of my plausible hypotheses?"

"This modification, this adjustment, I say, must have been done, and done quite well; done indeed for all 'Time', in the tremendous space of Time across which my machine had incredibly leapt. The air I breathed was free from gnats; the Earth apparently devoid of weeds, or fungi; everywhere were wonderful fruits and sweet and delightful flowers; brilliant butterflies harmlessly and safely flew about, hither and thither. The worthy ideal of producing preventive medicine had evidently been attained. Diseases, and lethal maladies, I suspected, had been efficaciously stamped-out. I saw no indications of any contagious diseases during all my stay among the dunce-like little people. And I shall have to tell you later in my story that even the processes of putrefaction and decay had been profoundly affected by these significant changes."

"Social triumphs, too, had evolved and had been deleteriously introduced to the detriment of the human race. I saw mankind housed in splendid shelters, gloriously clothed, and as yet, I had found them engaged in no toil or sacrifice. There were no signs of struggle, neither social nor economic rivalry. The shop; the advertisement; vehicle and wagon traffic; all that commerce which constitutes the body of *our* familiar busy world, was all gone. It was natural on that golden evening that I should jump at the idea of me entering a glorious social paradise. The difficulty of increasing population had been met, I guessed, and metropolitan and rural populations had ceased to increase."

"But with this radical change in condition comes inevitable adaptations to adjust to the radical change." 'What, unless biological science is a mass of errors, is the cause of human intelligence and vigor here in London?' I surmised. 'Hardship and freedom: conditions under which the active, strong, and subtle survive, and soon the weaker rely on government dependency; conditions that put a premium upon the loyal alliance of capable men; upon self-restraint, patience, and decision. And the institution of the family, and the emotions that arise therein; the fierce jealousy; the tenderness for affectionate offspring; parental self-devotion, all found their justification and support in the imminent dangers of the young."

"*Now*, where are these impending dangers that ensure progress and advancement in this ideal and idyllic age of the little people? There is a sentiment arising in 1899 London, and it will grow; an attitude against connubial jealousy; against fierce maternity; against the exhibition of passion and competition of all sorts; unnecessary things now, and things that make us feel uncomfortable, in our false idealistic pursuit of a refined, all-too-secure, and ultimately pleasant, fucked-up, societal life."

"I thought of the physical slightness of the future people, of their lack of intelligence, and of those big abundant ruins that existed in my midst, and it strengthened my belief in what resulted in a perfect conquest of Nature. For after the historic battle comes Quiet, Peace, and Tranquility. Humanity had been strong, energetic, competitive, and intelligent, and had used all its abundant vitality to alter the conditions under which it had lived and survived. And now, to my regret, came the reaction of the altered conditions; a grotesque reversal into cultural regression."

"Under the new conditions of perfect comfort and security, that restless energy, which had accompanied us in the form of strength, would degenerate into abject weakness. Even in our own time, certain tendencies and desires, once necessary to survival, are a constant source of failure. Physical courage and the love of battle, for instance, may even be hindrances, to an educated, idealistic, quixotic, civilized man. And in a state of physical balance and security, power, represented both as intellectual as well as physical potency, would be regarded as out of place. For countless years, I had judged that there had been no danger of war or solitary violence; no danger from wild beasts; no wasting disease to require strength of constitution, and no need of arduous toil. For such a life, what we should call the weak are as well-equipped as the strong; and therefore, are indeed no longer classified as weak. Better equipped indeed they are, for the strong would be fretted by an energy for which there was no outlet. No doubt the exquisite beauty of the buildings at which I had marveled was the outcome of the last surges of the now purposeless energy of mankind before it settled-down into perfect harmony with the conditions under which it had lived. This has ever been the fate of energy egregiously transformed into emotional security; an inspirational labor it takes to become productive in art, and then soon contaminates into eroticism, and thanks to Darwin's theory affecting the social situation of our times, after *that* transition, then perniciously evolves into ugly languor and decay."

"Even in *this* final-act, artistic impetus would at last die away, and had almost died-away in the flawed Future Time I had encountered. To adorn themselves with flowers, to dance, to sillily sing in the sunlight: so much was left of the former dynamic artistic spirit, and no more advancing or developing. Even that dimming creative facet would fade, in the end, into a devastating, contented inactivity. I maintain, gentlemen, that we are kept keen upon the grindstone of pain and necessity, and it seemed to me, contemplating all aspects of my weird visitation, that here was that hateful grindstone becoming shattered at last!"

"As I stood there relentlessly evaluating my circumstance in the gathering darkness, I gloomily thought that in this simple explanation I've just expounded, that I had mastered the existential problems of the world; indeed, had mastered the whole secret of these delicious, mentally fucked-up little people. Possibly the checks that their well-intentioned ancestors, us included, had devised for the increase of human population, and ostensibly, had succeeded all-too-well, and their numbers had rather diminished than kept at a favorable and stationary level. That logical explanation would account for the plethora of abandoned ruins. Very simple was my conclusive summary, and seemingly quite plausible enough, as most wrong theories ultimately are! But at that time, one assumption I had comprehended was that these little folk, lacking ambition and basic morality, but still, innocently dancing and prancing around in my midst, were too stupid to ever demonstrate any particular evil!"

Jay Dubya

Chapter 6

"A SUDDEN SHOCK"

"Now, my dear Doctor; you most-certainly are not a modern-day Hippocrates, who as we all are cognizant, was the ancient Greek Father of Medicine; and you, dear Editor, are no Edgar Allan Poe, the American magazine editor who is credited with being the Father of the Detective Story and of the classic Horror Story; and you, dear Psychologist, as your chosen field of study indicates; you certainly are not another Franz Mesmer, or a replica of that acclaimed German fellow, Sigmund Freud, who both happen to be major contributors to your Psychology field of endeavor. You three bored, phlegmatic listeners to my germane Time Machine thesis are only pedestrian practitioners of what other contributors to Western Civilization have already established and deftly developed! Your pathetic, mini-minds cannot comprehend that what I have produced, namely the Time Machine, is a major advancement in science, technology, not to mention world history!"

"Now, my dear friends, back to my important historical narrative. I had assumed that this 'New Fantasy World' I visited had an absence of malice and evil, but my original conjecture proved to be absolutely wrong. As I stood there musing over that all-too-perfect triumph of mankind, the full moon, yellow and gibbous, came-up out of an overflow of silver light in the northeast. The brightly clothed little figures ceased moving and meandering about below the hillside; a noiseless owl flitted-by, and my body began inexplicitly shivering with the chill of the sinister night approaching. I determined to descend and find where I could comfortably sleep."

"I looked for the cafeteria building I knew and trusted. Then, my keen vision traveled along the landscape to the figure of the White Sphinx, situated upon the pedestal of bronze, growing more distinct as the light of the rising moon grew brighter. In the background, I could see the high silver birch, touching against the odd structure's shoulder. There was again the tangle of rhododendron and hydrangea bushes, black in the pale light, and my keen eyes again recognized the familiar little lawn. I peered in astonishment at the lawn several times. A queer doubt chilled my foolish complacency. 'No!' I stoutly reckoned to myself. 'That was not the lawn. It can't be the same lawn'."

"But gentlemen; it indeed *was* the lawn. For the leprous, albino face of the White Sphinx was positioned towards the shrubbed meadow. Can you imagine what utter anxiety and complete apprehension I had felt as *that* awesome conviction came home to me? But you cannot imagine the total emotional impact. The indispensable Time Machine was gone! Missing in action!"

"At once, like a lash across my vulnerable face, came the distinct possibility of losing my anticipated return to my own age; a horrible feeling of then being left helpless, merely ineffectively existing in that strange new world. The bare thought of it was an actual, overwhelming, physical sensation. I could feel its alien power gripping me at the throat, and temporarily stopping my breathing."

"In another moment, my mind was possessed within a passion of heightened fear, and I found myself inadvertently running with great leaping strides down the adjacent slope. Once I fell and tumbled headlong, and accidentally cut my face upon a rock protruding from the dry turf; I lost no time in wiping-away the blood from my chin, but next, jumped-up and dashed-on, with a warm, scarlet trickle flowing-down my neck."

"All the while, I was dashing in fright and screaming to myself: 'The fucked-up little dunces have moved it a little; probably playfully pushing their new toy under nearby bushes, out of the way'."

"Nevertheless, at first, I speedily hustled with all my might, with no special destination in mind. All the time, with the certainty that sometimes comes with excessive dread, I knew that such frantic fantasy-behavior was folly; I instinctively knew that the machine had been egregiously removed out of my reach. My breathing was accompanied with heightening chest pain. I suppose I covered the whole distance from the hillside crest to the little lawn, two miles perhaps, in ten minutes. And I must emphasize the fact that I am *not* a young athletic man. Out of character, I cursed aloud, as I obsessively sprinted, and I condemned my stupid confidence in leaving the machine to the discretion of theft or confiscation. Surely, the little people were incapable of enacting a major prank, or for that matter, a simple joke or trick! I cried aloud, and no one answered. Not a creature seemed to be stirring, or even furtively maneuvering about in that ominous, moonlit world."

"When, in an exhausted state of mind and toting a beleaguered body, I finally reached the lawn upon which my Time Machine had landed; yes, my worst fears were realized. Not a trace of the 'escape mechanism' was to be seen. I felt faint and cold when I faced the empty space among the black tangle of bushes, realizing that I had been desperately trapped in that fucked-up future world. I dashed furiously around the Sphinx's perimeter several times, as if the machine might be hidden in a corner, and then stopped abruptly in my frenzy, with my bloody hands clutching, and soon pulling, my frazzled hair. Above me towered the mysterious White Sphinx, stationed and securely bolted upon the bronze pedestal; its face white, shining, leprous; prominently and permanently anchored in the light of the rising moon. Truthfully, my frightened perception was that the strange monument seemed to be derisively smiling in evil mockery at my emotional dismay."

"I absurdly consoled myself by imagining that the brain-dead little people had safeguarded the mechanism by putting it in some protective shelter, had I not felt certain of their physical and intellectual inadequacy. That is precisely what had rattled and freaked me out: the sense of some hitherto, unsuspected power, through whose intervention my invention had mystically vanished."

"Yet, for one essential matter, I felt assured: unless some other age had produced its exact duplicate, the machine could not have, all by itself, moved in time. The attachment of the levers, I will show you the method later, prevented anyone from tampering with my apparatus when the operating controls had been sagely removed from the instrument panel. 'My machine had been moved, and was hidden, only in space. But then, where could it be concealed? 'And who or what could have moved it'?"

"I think I must have then experienced a kind of tremendous panic attack. I remember running violently in and out among the dense, moonlit bushes, again, in a neurotic, paranoid manner, sprinting all around the White Sphinx, and startling some white animal that, in the dim light, I mistook for a small deer. I remember, too, late that night, beating the bushes with my clenched fists until my knuckles were gashed and bleeding from incessantly banging my clenched fists against the broken twigs."

"Then, sobbing and raving in my ascending anguish, I frantically hurried-down to the great building of stone. The big cafeteria hall was dark, silent, and deserted. I slipped and tripped upon the uneven floor, and awkwardly fell over one of the slate-top tables, almost breaking my right shin. I frenetically lit a match and slowly wandered-on, cautiously stepping past the stench-laden, dusty curtains, of which I have previously described."

"There, in the illumination of my lit match, I discovered a second great hall with its floor covered with cushions, upon which, perhaps, a score or so of the little people were innocently sleeping. I have no doubt that the dozers found my 'second intrusion' being unexpected and disturbing enough, with me suddenly arriving out of the quiet darkness, making distinct, inarticulate noises, and employing the splutter and flare of a match. For quite obviously, I fathomed that the mindless dunces had forgotten about matches."

Both my rational mind and my emotions were captured in a swirling, mental maelstrom. 'Where is my Time Machine?' I wondered, bawling like an angry child, and then laying my hands upon the frightened and victimized little people in my presence, and next wildly shaking them up, and thereafter, flinging them about like ragdolls in the darkness. That encounter must've been very queer and upsetting to their underdeveloped psyches. Some of the fucked-up idiots laughed, but as I scratched and lit my second match, most of the dumb-shits looked sorely frightened at my aggressive activity. When I noticed the dolts standing around me like complete morons, it came into my addled head that I was performing a foolish reaction, under the dire circumstances, in trying to revive the sensation of fear in those inferior ignoramuses. For, reasoning and concluding from their daylight behavior, I thought that over the millenniums, emotional fear must have been forgotten."

"Abruptly, I dashed-down the match, and knocking one of the tiny people over in my haste, I reversed my path and went blundering in the dark across the big dining-hall again, and impatiently stepped-out under the moonlight. I heard multiple cries of terror, and listened to the sound of *their* little feet running and stumbling in the vicinity, this way and that."

"I do not remember all I did as the moon dismally and ominously crept-up the night sky. I suppose it was the unexpected nature of my loss that maddened me to the brink of insanity. I felt hopelessly cut-off from my own human kind; I felt like a strange animal trapped in an unknown, hostile world. I must've raved and scurried about for several hours, scampering to-and-fro, screaming, cursing, and crying upon God and Fate."

"In retrospect, gentlemen, I have a memory of suffering horrible fatigue, as the long night of despair and worry wore away; my weary eyes futilely searched all over *that* impossible, dark environment. I recollect me groping among moonlit ruins, and my wary fingers touching strange creatures hiding in the black shadows. At last, I recall lying upon the ground near the White Sphinx, and continuously weeping with absolute wretchedness; my consciousness being ever-angry at the folly of leaving my indispensable machine vulnerable and unattended. I had nothing left but to endure insufferable misery. Then, out of great fatigue, I slept, and when I eventually awoke, it was full day, and a couple of innocuous sparrows were fearlessly hopping around me upon the turf, within reach of my arm."

"I sat-up in the freshness of the morning, attempting to remember how I had gotten there, and why I was feeling such a profound sense of desolation and despair. Then, negative memories came clearly focused into my troubled mind. With the plain, reasonable daylight, I could lucidly look my circumstances fairly in the face. I recollected the wildness of my overnight ordeal, and I could better rationally reason with myself. 'Suppose the worst?' I considered. 'Suppose the machine is altogether lost; perhaps destroyed? It behooves me to be calm and objectively patient; there must be more to this alien world than originally has met my eyes; I need to learn the total habits of the mentally-challenged little people, so that I can get a clearer idea of the method of my loss, and then possibly obtain the means of getting necessary materials and tools; so that in the end, perhaps fortuitously, I may manufacture another Time Machine'."

"That favorable result would be my only hope, in reality, a poor hope, perhaps; but in a positive sense, much better than accepting despair. And, after all, it was a beautiful and curious world I had accidentally discovered."

"But quite possibly, the machine had only been temporarily taken-away. Still, I must be calm and patient; find its hiding-place, and recover the vital device by either force or by cunning. And with that inspirational notion, I scrambled to my feet and looked about me, wondering where I could wash and bathe. Naturally, I felt weary, stiff, and travel-soiled."

"The freshness of the morning made me desire and achieve an equal freshness. I had exhausted both my emotions and my mental capacity. Indeed, as I went about my investigative business, I found myself wondering at my intense excitement that prevailed during my overnight misadventure. I made a careful examination of the ground about the little lawn, and I wasted some time engaging-in futile interrogations of the little people, whom I randomly confronted. The dumb-shit idiots all failed to understand my alien gestures; some were simply stolid; while others of the fucked-up species thought my hand motions were mere comical jests, and subsequently, the lackluster dunces laughed at me."

"I had the hardest task in the world keeping my bleeding hands off their pretty, laughing faces, and then severely and violently injuring their delicate countenances. Pummeling the little twerps was a foolish impulse that I needed to control. Scrutinizing the turf, however, offered me better counsel. I noticed parallel deep grooves ripped into the grass, about midway between the pedestal of the sphinx and the marks of my feet where, on arrival, I had struggled with the overturned machine."

"There were other signs of ground disturbance, with queer, narrow footprints, similar to those I could imagine made by an errant sloth. This alert observation directed my closer attention to the bronze pedestal, which was not a mere solid block, but highly decorated with deep, framed panels on either side. I gathered courage and rapped loudly at those closed portals, and soon discovered that the pedestal was indeed hollow."

"Examining the panels with greater care, I found them to be discontinuous with the frames. There were no handles or keyholes, but possibly the panels, if they were functional doors, as I supposed, opened from within. One thing was clear enough to my fascinated mind. It took no very great mental effort to infer that my essential Time Machine had been stashed inside that sinister pedestal. But how it had gotten inside was a different problem to consider."

"I saw the heads of two orange-clad people coming through the bushes and bobbing under several blossom-covered apple-like-trees, heading directly towards me. I turned and smiled, beckoning for the 'flower children' to approach me. Pointing to the bronze pedestal, I tried to intimate my strong wish to open it. But at my first gesture towards that symbolic suggestion, the tiny cretins behaved very oddly."

"I don't know how to exactly convey their astonished expression to you. Suppose you were to use a grossly improper gesture, like giving the middle finger to an anonymous, straightlaced, delicate-minded, Victorian woman; it is exactly how she would look, her facial expression being rather appalled. The dumb-ass tiny jerk-offs, if indeed the whimsical fools knew how to work their puny dick-sticks, all wandered-off as if the deficient simpletons had received the maximal possible insult."

"Next, I tried questioning a sweet-looking little chap dressed in white, with my emphatic efforts attaining exactly the same ignorant result. Somehow, his manner made me feel ashamed of myself for abruptly interfering with his phony happiness. But, as you well-know, I desperately wanted the Time Machine, and I tried communicating with the dunderhead once more. As the dumb-shit swiftly turned-away, just like the others, my temper got the better of me. In three strides, I was scurrying after his tiny ass; grabbed the dimwit by the loose part of his robe, and I roughly twisted the fabric around the dumb-fuck's neck, and began dragging the bawling knucklehead towards the sphinx. Then, I saw the horror and repugnance upon his scared-shitless face, and all of a sudden, I let him go about his daily play."

"But, however, my determination was not yet beaten. I banged with my already-abused fists against the corroded bronze panels. I thought I heard something stir inside; to be more explicit, I believed that I had heard a sound like a subtle chuckle; but I considered that I must have been mistaken. Then, I picked-up a big rock from the nearby river, and savagely hammered the bronze portals until I had flattened a coil in the decorations, and the accumulated rust came off in powdery flakes."

"The delicate little people must have heard me pounding-away in gusty outbreaks a full mile in all directions, but nothing tangible ever resulted from my vigorous enterprise. I saw a crowd of the midget-assholes gathering upon the elevated slopes, looking furtively at my demonstration of frustration. At last, hot and tired, I sat-down to visually analyze the general environment. But I was too restless to watch for long; I am too Occidental to patiently contemplate matters for a long vigil. I could work at a problem for years, but to wait and be inactive for twenty-four hours without getting any satisfactory results, well, that dilemma is another matter."

"I got-up to my aching feet after a time, and began walking aimlessly through the bushes towards the aforementioned hillside again. 'Patience,' I reckoned to myself. 'If you want your machine again, you must leave that imposing sphinx alone. If they, whoever the hell 'they' are, mean to take your machine away, it's little good of you wrecking their bronze panels, and if they don't, you will get it back as soon as you can ask, or possibly diplomatically negotiate for it. To sit amongst all those unknown alien structures and monuments, evaluating such a perplexing puzzle like the missing Time Machine, I reckoned, was positively hopeless. That way lies complete monomania. Face this indecipherable world with measured courage and conviction. Learn its peculiar ways; watch it, and be careful of imagining too hastily erroneous guesses about its exact meaning. In the end, you will eventually find clues to explain it all'."

"Then, suddenly the general humor of the whole situation entered into my mind: the thought of the years I had spent in study and toil to travel into *that* convoluted future age, and now my passion of anxiety to rapidly get the hell out of it. I had made myself the most complicated, and the most hopeless trap, that ever a man could devise. Although it was at my own expense, I could not help myself. I laughed aloud at my utter haplessness and total ignorance."

"Going again through the colossal eating and sleeping palace, the edifice being a combination cafeteria and dormitory, it seemed to me that the little people intentionally avoided my presence. It may have been my fancy, or it may have had something to do with my violent hammering at the gates of bronze. Yet, I felt tolerably sure of their deliberate avoidance. I was careful, however, to show them no worry or concern, and also, to abstain from any pursuit of their ivory-white asses, and in the course of a day or two, things finally would get back to their old footing."

"I made what progress I could in mastering their simple language, and in addition, I doggedly pushed my explorations here and there in all four directions. Either I missed some subtle point, or their asinine language was excessively rudimentary, almost exclusively composed of concrete nouns and action verbs, both of which showed little abstract qualities, or any indications of figurative or creative language."

"Their vague sentences were usually quite simplistic, and mostly consisted of only two words, and I failed to ever recognize the little imbeciles' comprehension of collective nouns, of pronouns, of adjectives, of adverbs, or even of basic prepositions. I determined to put the memory of my missing Time Machine, and the mystery of the bronze doors located under the White Sphinx, as much as possible, in a far corner of my brain; that was, until my growing knowledge would lead me back to those considerations in a more natural and rational way. Yet, a certain feeling, you may appreciate and understand, tethered me in a circle of a few miles around the original point of my arrival."

Chapter 7

"EXPLANATION"

"So, as far as I could determine, all the world displayed the same exuberant richness as the future Thames valley had shown. From every hill I climbed, I observed the same abundance of splendid buildings, endlessly varied in material and style; the same clustering thickets of evergreens; the same blossom-laden trees and lower tree fern-type growths. Here and there, water streams and creeks shone like silver, and beyond, the land rose into blue, undulating hills, and so majestically faded into the serenity of the sky."

"A peculiar feature, which presently attracted my attention, as I have previously alluded, was the presence of certain circular wells; several, as it seemed, of a very great depth. One lay by the path up the hill which I had followed during my first area trek. Like the others, it was rimmed with bronze, curiously wrought, and protected by a little, slanted-roof cupola from the rainfall. Sitting by the side of these wells, and peering-down into the shafted darkness, I could see no gleam of water, nor could I start any reflection with a lighted match."

"But in all of the vertical holes, my ears discerned a certain dull sound: a rhythmic thud—thud—thud; the repetitious noise almost-simulating the low-beating of some hulking engine. And performing a little experiment, I discovered, from the flaring of my matches, that a steady current of air drifted-down the shafts. Further, I tossed a scrap of paper into the throat of one, and, instead of fluttering slowly-down, it was at once sucked swiftly out of sight."

"After a time, too, I came to connect these wells with tall towers standing here and there, that dotted upon the region's slopes; for above them, there was often just such a flicker into the air as one sees on a hot day above a sun-scorched beach. Putting things together, my mind reached a strong suggestion of an extensive system of subterranean ventilation, whose true import it was difficult for my limited cerebrum to even imagine. I was at first inclined to associate these assorted objects with the sanitary apparatus of these illiterate little people. But obviously, that was an erroneous conclusion, since the small folk had no knowledge or concept of industry, factories, or physical work."

"And here, I must admit that I had learned very little of sewage drains, and of steeple bells, along with various modes of conveyance, during my confusing tenure in that all-too-real future. In some of these 1899 visions of Utopias and coming times, which I have read from ample academic 'Sociology' journal articles, there is a vast amount of detail about futuristic buildings, and a variety of advanced social arrangements, and so forth. But while such details are easy enough to obtain when the whole world is contained in one's imagination, the impressions are altogether inaccessible to an aspiring 1899 Time Traveler, amid such realities as I had found in the distant future."

"Now, my friends; try and conceive of the perceptions of an astounded jungle native, visiting modern London, and freshly arrived from Central Africa; just imagine the memories that he or she would take back to his or her tribe! What would he or she know of railway companies, of social movements, of telephone and telegraph wires, of the Parcel Delivery Company, and of postal orders and the like? Yet we, at least, should be willing enough to explain these things to him! And even of what he or she knew, how much could he or she make his or her untraveled friends, back in Africa, either apprehend or actually believe?"

"In the matter of cemeteries, and of grave monuments, for instance; I could see no signs of crematoria, nor any suggestive signs of tombs. But it occurred to me that, possibly, there might be cemeteries (or crematoria) somewhere beyond the range of my daytime exploring. My thought processes, and my curiosity, were stifled and thwarted in my conjecturing about a certain consideration. The thing that truly confounded my reasoning, and I was led to make a further mental note, which puzzled me still more: that aged and infirm among this weird people there were none. Had science discovered nectar and ambrosia? Had human immortality finally been achieved?"

"I must confess that my satisfaction with my first theories of an automatic civilization evolving into a lazy, decadent humanity, did not long endure. Yet I could think of no other explanatory accounting. Let me put my difficulties into precise vernacular. The several big palaces I had explored were mere living places, great dining-halls, and convenient mass sleeping apartments. I could find no machinery, no appliances, no functional technology of any kind. Yet these doltish people were clothed in pleasant fabrics that must at times need renewal, and their sandals, though undecorated, were fairly complex specimens of leather and metalwork. Somehow, such things must be meticulously manufactured. And these little folks seemed incapable of growing and providing the fruit inside their large cafeteria red bowls!"

"And furthermore, the dumb-ass little people displayed no vestige of possessing or showing any creative tendency. There were no shops, no workshops, no retail stores, no schools or universities, and no sign of importations among the entire society. The short, frumpy assholes spent all their time in gently dancing-around like nursery school children; and throwing flowers; in merrily bathing in the nearby river; in making love in a half-playful fashion; in eating fruit, and in sleeping. Those unproductive activities constituted their daily schedule. I could not see how things were kept going."

"Then, again, about the Time Machine: something, I knew not what, had to have a degree of intelligence, or cunning, and had mischievously pushed and dragged the mechanism into the hollow pedestal of the White Sphinx. *Why?* For the life of me, I could not imagine the underlying motive. Those waterless wells, too, were indiscernible, along with those inexplicable flickering pillars. I felt I lacked a breakthrough clue as to identifying their true significance. I felt, how shall I put it? Suppose you found an inscription, with sentences here and there in excellent plain English, and with strange symbols etched therein, and others made-up of indecipherable words; of letters even, or perhaps Egyptian hieroglyphics or ancient cuneiform, all abstract figures absolutely unknown to you? Well, on the third day of my visit into the far future, that was exactly how the world of Eight Hundred and Two Thousand Seven Hundred and One presented itself to me!"

"That third day, too, I made a female friend, of a sort. It happened that, as I was watching some of the little people bathing in a shallow, crystal-blue stream, one of the waders was seized with cramp, and began drifting and screaming downstream. The main current ran rather swiftly, but not too strongly for even a moderate swimmer to conquer. It will give you an idea, therefore, of the strange deficiency existing in these delicate creatures, when I tell you that none of the spectators made the slightest attempt at rescuing the weakly crying little female, who was drowning, thrashing about, and screaming before their very eyes."

"When I realized this uncanny set of circumstances, I hurriedly slipped-off my outer clothes, and, wading in at a point lower downstream, I caught the poor mite and drew her safely to land. A little rubbing of the limbs soon brought the petite blonde survivor around to normal respiration, and I had the satisfaction of seeing that she was all right before I left her company without ever receiving a casual 'Thank you'. I had arrived at such a low estimation of her kind that I did not expect to receive any special gratitude from her. In that respect, however, I was proven wrong."

"This almost-tragic event happened in the early morning. In the afternoon, I again met my little woman, as I believe it was, when I was returning towards my central base near the White Sphinx from exercising a general exploration. My cute little lady friend received me with cries of delight, and eagerly presented me with a big garland of flowers, evidently especially made for me, and me alone. The idea of me receiving a gift from one of those little imps took my imagination by surprise."

"Very possibly, I had been feeling desolate. At any rate, I did my best to display my appreciation of the small token of gratitude. We were soon seated together in a narrow stone arbor, engaged in primitive conversation, chiefly of smiles and gestures. The creature's friendliness affected me exactly as a child's might have done after being doted upon. We passed each other flowers, and she kissed my hands. Being impressed, I did the same to hers. Then, I tried talking, and found that her name was Weena, which, although I don't know exactly what it meant, the odd appellation somehow seemed appropriate enough. That was the beginning of a peculiar friendship which lasted for almost a week, and dramatically ended as I will soon reveal to you!"

"Weena behaved exactly like a child of *our'* times. She wanted to be with me always, following me everywhere, and on my next journey out and about, it went to my heart to tire her down, and leave her at last, exhausted and calling after me rather plaintively. But in *my* very determined mind, the problems of the world had to be mastered."

"I had not ventured into the future to carry-on a miniature flirtation with a young girl having a toddler's mentality. Yet, her obvious distress when I left her alone was very great, for Weena's emotional grief at our partings was sometimes frantic, and I think that I had as much trouble as I had comfort from her daily devotion."

"My usual keen and dependable instinct thought that it was mere childish affection that made her automatically cling to me. Until it was too late, I did not clearly know what I had inflicted upon her when I foolishly left her by herself. Nor until it was too late, did I fully understand what her immature company had meant to my disconsolate spirit. For, by merely seeming fond of my presence, and showing in her weak, futile way that she cared for my existence, the little doll of a creature presently gave my return to the neighborhood of the White Sphinx, almost the feeling of coming home after a long separation; and I would watch for her tiny figure garbed in white and gold material as soon as I came strolling over the familiar hill."

"It was from her, too, that I learned that anxiety had not yet left the future world. Weena was fearless enough in the daylight, and she had the oddest confidence in me; for once, in a foolish moment, I made threatening grimaces at her, and the pretty blonde girl simply laughed at my frowning facial expressions. But my little friend dreaded the dark, dreaded shadows, and dreaded black things. Darkness to her was the one experience that absolutely terrified her. It was a singularly passionate emotion, and it set my mind thinking, and my suspicious eyes observing."

"I discovered then that these little people gathered into the great houses after dark, and for security, slept in droves. To enter upon their slumbers without a light was to send the miniature dolts into a tumult of extreme apprehension. I never found one dozing out of doors, or one ever sleeping alone within doors, after dark. Yet, I was still such a thick-skulled blockhead that I missed the essential lesson of that fear, and in spite of Weena's pouting distress, I insisted upon sleeping away from these slumbering, dimwitted multitudes."

"My absence and need for independence troubled her greatly, but in the end, Weena's odd affection triumphed, and for five of the nights of our wonderful acquaintance, including the last night of all, she slept with her fair head pillowed upon my arm. But my story slips away from me as I speak of her."

"Now gentlemen, it must have been the night before her rescue from drowning that I had been awakened about dawn. I had been restless, dreaming most disagreeably that I had been drowned, and that hostile sea anemones were feeling over my face with their soft palps. I woke with a jolting startle, and my fuzzy senses perceived an odd fancy that some greyish animal had just rushed-out of the dormitory chamber. I tried to get back to sleep again, but I felt extremely restless and especially uncomfortable. It was that dim grey twilight hour when things are just creeping-out of darkness; when everything is colorless and clear cut, and yet both visually unreal and surreal. I got-up from the hard stone floor, and ambled-down into the great hall, and thereafter trekked-out upon the flagstones in front of the huge palace. I thought I would make a virtue out of necessity, and marvel at seeing a magnificent sunrise."

"The moon was setting, and its dying light, along with the first pallor of dawn, were mingled in a ghastly half-illumination. The surrounding bushes were inky black; the ground a very somber grey, and the changing sky then colorless and cheerless. And up the hill, I thought I could see a contingent of scampering ghosts. Three times, as I scanned the slope, my eyes noticed white figures scurrying-around in zealous haste. Twice I fancied I saw a solitary white, ape-like creature running rather quickly up the hill, and once again near the bent aluminum ruins. My eyes observed, and my ears heard, a squealing party of these new fleeting beings carrying some dark body. The apparitions seemed to move-about rapidly, as to avoid passing a deadline. I did not see what became of the peculiar creatures after the company disappeared over the nearby knoll. It seemed that the 'white-furred animals' had vanished among the myriad bushes and shrubs. The sky's dawn was still indistinct, you must understand. I was feeling that unnerving chill; that uncertain, early-morning feeling you may have known in your early morning perception. And so, I doubted my eyes, and also questioned my brain's incredulous comprehension."

"As the eastern sky grew brighter, and the light of morning came-on, and its vivid coloring returned upon the world once more, I scanned the view very keenly. But I saw no vestige of the rushing white figures that were haunting my recollection. 'They must have been imagined ghosts, or twilight illusions or apparitions,' I theorized. 'If each successive generation dies and leave ghosts, the world, over thousands and thousands of evolving years, will become overcrowded with flitting specters. On that wild theory, the apparitions would have grown innumerable some Eight Hundred Thousand Years hence, and it was no great wonder to see four flitting shades scurrying-about at once."

"But my imaginative jest was unsatisfying, and I was objectively thinking of those nebulous white figures all that morning, until Weena's rescue from drowning had driven their images out of my head. I associated the white ghosts, in some indefinite way, with the white animal hiding in the bushes that I had startled in my first passionate search for the missing Time Machine."

Jay Dubya

"Now gentlemen, I think I have stated how much hotter than our own 1899 temperature was the weather of this mystifying Golden Age. Even now, I cannot entirely account for it. It may be that the sun was hotter, or perhaps the Earth had moved nearer the sun. It is usual for the scientifically-educated mind to assume that the sun will go on cooling steadily in the future. But people, unfamiliar with such speculations as those of the younger Darwin, forget that the planets must ultimately fall back one by one into the parent solar body. As these catastrophes occur, the sun will blaze with renewed energy; and it may be that some inner planet, maybe Mercury or Venus, had suffered this fate of sacrificing itself to *our* nearest star."

"Well, one very hot morning, my fourth, I think, as I was seeking shelter from the heat and glare inside a colossal ruin near the great cafeteria/dormitory house where I had slept and fed, there happened this strange occurrence. Clambering among these jagged heaps of masonry, I found a narrow gallery, whose end and side windows were blocked by fallen masses of stone. By contrast with the brilliancy outside, it seemed to me at first impenetrably dark inside. I entered the aperture, methodically groping-around with my arms and hands, for the change from light to blackness made spots of color swim before my affected pupils. Suddenly, I halted my investigation, with my shocked mind being spellbound. A pair of opposite red eyes, luminous by reflection, had been surreptitiously watching me out of the interior darkness."

"The old instinctive dread of savage and vicious wild beasts inherently came upon me. I clenched my fists and steadfastly stared into adversarial, glaring eyeballs, and naturally, I was quite afraid to turn my back. Then, the thought of the absolute daylight security in which humanity appeared to be living came to my mind. And next, I remembered that strange terror that Weena had associated with the dark."

"Overcoming my fear to some extent, I advanced a step forward and intrepidly spoke in a hoarse voice that was harsh and ill-controlled. I extended my hand and touched something soft. At once, the eyes of that unknown creature darted sideways, and quickly, something white sped past me in the partial darkness. I turned with my heart rising to my throat, and my dilated pupils perceived a queer, chest-high, ape-like figure, whose presence had emitted a terrible stench. The newly-discovered life-form blundered against a block of granite, staggered aside, and in a brief moment, was hidden in a black shadow beneath another obscure pile of rubble."

"My impression of the fleeting animal was, of course, imperfect; but I had recognized that its fur was a dull white, and the odd mobile manifestation had strange-large, greyish-red eyes. Also, there was thick, flaxen hair upon its head, and growing in abundance straight down its back. But, as I say, 'the white ape' zipped-away too fast for me to distinctly see its entire form. I cannot even reveal whether it ran on all fours, or only with its forearms held very low like a gorilla or chimpanzee."

"After an instant's pause, I gathered my wits and boldly followed the furry creature into the second heap of ruins. I could not find it at first; but, after a time searching inside the profound obscurity, I furtively entered one of those rounded, *well openings* of which I have told you, half-closed by a fallen pillar. A sudden thought came to my awareness. Could this 'Thing' have vanished and escaped my scrutiny down the shaft?"

"I lit a match, and, peering-down below, I noticed a small, white, descending creature, with large bright red eyes, which regarded me steadfastly as it methodically retreated. The grotesque-looking little monster made my body shudder. It was so much like a disgusting human spider! The small Simian was clambering-down the well's sidewall, and then I saw for the first time a number of metal foot and hand rests, or rungs, forming a kind of underground ladder down the shaft. Soon, the match's light burned my fingers, and fell, burning-out as it dropped, and when I had lit another flame, the little monster had stealthily disappeared below."

"I do not know how long I sat peering-down that vertical well tunnel. The hideous thing that my eyes had seen was definitely not human. But gradually, the truth dawned upon me: Mankind had not remained one species, but had differentiated into two distinct animals: the graceful children of the Upper World were not the sole descendants of our generation, but that this bleached, obscene, nocturnal, gruesome Thing, which had surreptitiously flashed before me, was also heir to all the ages."

"I thought of the flickering pillars, and of my theory of an underground ventilation system. Soon, I began to suspect their true import. And what, I wondered, was this mysterious 'Lemur' doing in my scheme of a perfectly balanced organization? How was 'it' related to the indolent serenity of the beautiful Over-worlders? And what was hidden down there, at the foot of that cryptic shaft? I sat upon the edge of the well, telling myself that I must descend into the dark shaft to discover the solution of my numerous difficulties. And with *that* horrid realization, I was absolutely afraid to begin a pursuit! As I hesitated, two of the beautiful-but-fucked-up upperworld people came running in their amorous sport across the daylight and into the shadow. The sex-driven male was frivolously pursuing the female, affectionately flinging flowers at her as the dumb-shit scampered and chased."

"The pair hesitated in their activity, stopped abruptly, and seemed distressed to find me there, with my arm leaning against the overturned pillar, peering-down into the well. When I pointed to the well's opening, and tried to frame a question about it in their native tongue, the duo became even more visibly distressed, and immediately turned away. But the twosome was extremely interested by the glow of my matches, and I struck two more to amuse their' fascination. I tried asking the pair a second time about the enigmatic well, and again, my attempt failed."

"So presently, I left them to resume their sexual courting, meaning to go back to Weena, and see what constructive information my questioning could derive from her. But my mind was already in convulsive revolution; my guesses and impressions were slipping and sliding to formulate a new adjustment. I had now a clue to the import of those arcane wells; to the relative 'ventilating towers'; to the mystery of the fleeting ghosts; to say nothing of a hint at the meaning of the bronze gates, and the related fate of the pilfered and concealed Time Machine! And very vaguely, there came a strong suggestion towards the solution of the economic problem that had puzzled me. Those deplorable ape-like creatures were to become my avowed enemies!"

"Now gentlemen, here was my new view of that fucked-up, oddball, future age. Plainly, this second species of 'Man's Descendants' was subterranean. There were three circumstances in particular which made me think that the Thing's rare emergence above ground was the outcome of a long-continued underground habit. In the first scenario, there was the bleached look common in most animals that live largely in the dark; the white fish of the famous Kentucky caves, for instance. Then, those large eyes, with their capacity for reflecting light, are common features of nocturnal animals, as evidenced in the hunting owl and the predator cat. And last of all, that ape-like monster's general confusion in the sunshine; yes, that hasty-yet-fumbling awkward flight towards dark shadow, and that peculiar carrying of the crestfallen head while clumsily staggering-about in the daylight, all reinforced the theory of an extreme sensitiveness of the white ape's retinas."

"Beneath my feet, then, the Earth must be tunneled enormously, and these excavations were the habitat of the divergent 'New Race'. The presence of ventilating shafts and wells along the hill slopes, evident everywhere, in fact, except along the river valley, showed how universal were its ramifications. This extraordinary dichotomy, or splitting of the human species, made me think extensively as to how the two species were interacting. And did these two species have separate names?"

"At first, gentlemen, this is what I had hypothesized. I surmised that the Capitalist and the Laborer were the keys to my whole supposition. No doubt, it will seem grotesque enough to you, and certainly wildly incredible! And yet, even now, there are existing circumstances to point that way. There is a tendency to utilize underground space for the less ornamental purposes of modern civilization. For graphic example, as you know, there is the Metropolitan Railway in London; and there are new electric railways called subways. And we also boast of underground workrooms and restaurants, and their numbers increase and multiply with each passing year. Evidently, industry had gradually lost its birthright above ground. I mean, that factories had gone deeper and deeper into larger and ever larger underground facilities, spending a still-increasing amount of its time in a subterranean setting. Even now in 1899, do not East-end workers, not to mention coal miners, live in such artificial conditions as practically to be cut-off from the natural surface of the Earth?"

"Again, the exclusive tendency of richer people, no doubt, due to the increasing refinement of their education, and also due to the widening gulf between them and the Proletarians, along with the rude ghetto violence of the poor, is already leading to the closing of considerable portions of the surface of the land. About London, for instance, perhaps half the prettier country is shut-in against industrial intrusion. And this same widening gulf between factory owners and factory workers is ever-expanding."

"So, in the end, above ground you must have the wealthy 'Haves', pursuing pleasure, comfort and beauty, and below ground, the unfortunate 'Have-nots'; the indigent Workers getting continually adapted to the poor conditions of their daily labor. Once the lowly Under-grounders became adapted to subterranean conditions, the poorer inhabitants would no doubt have to pay rent and pay for the ventilation of their caverns; and if the laborers refused, they would starve or be suffocated into bankruptcy for being in arrears. The underground dwellers would either have to evolve and adapt, or suffer dire consequences in either prison or workhouses. In other words, everything beautiful and lazy remained above ground, and everything ugly and miserable was conversely pushed beneath the Earth."

"The great triumph of Humanity which I had naively dreamed of had taken a different shape inside my limited-in-scope comprehension. Instead, I imagined that a real Aristocracy, armed with perfected science and industrial technology, and that *this* resulting elite wealthy class had been working toward a logical conclusion, which was the culmination of the exploitive factory system of today. Its triumph had not been simply a victory over Nature, but a triumph over Nature along with the Under-world fellow man. This, I must warn you, was my theory at that time."

"My explanation may be absolutely wrong, but I still think that it is the most plausible one. But even on interpreting *this* radical supposition, the balanced civilization that was at last attained must have long since passed its zenith, and had in the distant future fallen into total decay. The too-perfect security of the Over-worlders had led them to a slow movement of eventual cultural degeneration; yes, to a general dwindling in size, strength, and intelligence. That I could see clearly enough already. What exactly had happened to the furry Undergrounders, I did not yet suspect; but, from what I had seen of the 'Morlocks', for that was the name by which these ape-like creatures were called by Weena, who also, when questioned, identified the 'Eloi,' as the beautiful-but-childish race that I already knew and had a low opinion of."

"Then, to my suspicious mind came rather troublesome doubts. Why had the Morlocks taken my precious Time Machine? For I felt sure that it was the ugly white apes who had purloined it. If the Eloi were the rich masters, why could they not restore the machine to me? And why were they so terribly afraid of the dark? I proceeded to intensively question Weena about this new-found Underworld culture, but here again I was vastly disappointed."

"At first, my Eloi little woman would not understand my questions, and presently, she refused to even attempt answering the inquiries. Weena shivered as though the topic was unendurable, and positively forbidden to even be considered. And when I pressed her on the subject, perhaps a little too harshly, she incidentally burst into tears. Hers were the only tears, except my own, that I ever saw shed in that fucked-up Golden Age. I ceased interrogating her about the indigenous-and-eerie Morlock sons-of-bitches. And very soon, my little female companion was again smiling and clapping her hands, while I solemnly entertained her by foolishly burning and squandering another precious match.

Jay Dubya

Chapter 8

"THE MORLOCKS"

"Now gentlemen, naturally I had decided to side with Weena and the petite-but-airheaded Eloi against the seemingly despicable Morlocks. I even joked in one of my whimsical moments of thinking that the vulnerable Eloi should have 'more locks' on their doors as a security protection against the deplorable ape-like, white-furred monsters."

"My curious brain was considering how the Future World had abandoned our traditional institutions such as schools, hospitals, churches, temples, synagogues, organized government, economic systems, bartering by using money, transportation systems, police and fire departments, brothels, bordellos, whorehouses, legal, courts, prisons, agricultural bureaus, nudist colonies, sex camps, above ground factories, retail stores, post offices, along with railroad trains, paved avenues and wide boulevards."

"And even today in the Year 1899, there is grumbling going on in Russia about the czar's monarchy being upended by a Marxist/Socialist Revolution. Such an uprising would preclude the future scenario from happening where the human race would diverge into the Eloi and the Morlock civilizations, because the industrial workers, known as the Proletarians, would rebel against the elite czarist/nobility class, known as the Aristocracy, thus keeping all human activity above ground, and avoiding a subterranean class such as the future Morlocks from ever evolving. This, at least, was my assessment and speculation that is now worthy of your concern and attention."

"However, it may seem odd to you, but it was two days before I could follow-up the new-found clue in what was manifestly the proper method of attack to pursue. I felt a peculiar shrinking from those sickening, pallid bodies. The stench-laden Morlocks were just the half-bleached color of the worms one sees preserved in formaldehyde, on display in a zoological museum. And the sinister apes were filthily cold to the touch. Probably my physical shrinking and my mental shirking were largely due to the sympathetic influence of the defenseless Eloi, whose observable disgust of the Morlocks I now began to amply appreciate. But despite my reluctance, I knew that I should soon take appropriate action against the gruesome adversaries."

"The next night, I tossed and turned upon the hard dormitory floor, and did not sleep well. Probably my mental and physical health was a little disordered. My mind was oppressed with accumulative perplexity and mounting doubt. Once or twice, I had a feeling of intense fear enveloping me, for which I could perceive no definite reason. I remember creeping noiselessly into the great hall where the little people were sleeping, with the moonlight penetrating though the open windows. That night Weena was among her little comrades, and apparently feeling reassured by their presence. It occurred to me, even then, that in the course of a few days, the moon must predictably pass through its last quarter, and the nights would grow darker, when the appearances of these unpleasant creatures from below, these whitened-Lemurs, this new-vermin that had replaced the obsolete rats and mice, might be more active and abundant."

"And on both those days, I had the restless feeling of one who evades an inevitable duty, or should I say 'responsibility'. I felt assured that the Time Machine was only to be recovered by me boldly penetrating those mysteries of the underground culture, or lack thereof. Yet, I could not audaciously face the imminent mystery. If only I had had an 1899 companion, perhaps one of you, my noble resolve would have been so very different. But I was so horribly alone, and even to clamber-down into the darkness of the designated well, the aspiration appalled me to the point where I felt nauseous and about to vomit. I don't know if you will understand my irregular feeling, but I never felt quite safe at my back."

"It was this persistent restlessness, that enveloping insecurity, perhaps, which drove me farther and farther afield in my exploring expeditions. Going to the south-westward direction towards the rising country that is now called Combe Wood, I observed far-off, in the direction of nineteenth-century Banstead, a vast green structure, different in character from any I had hitherto seen. The fabulous edifice was larger than the largest of the palaces or ruins that I had observed or visited, and the jade façade had a distinct Oriental look: the face of it having the luster, as well as a pale-green tint, a kind of bluish-green, of a certain type of Chinese porcelain. This difference in appearance suggested a difference in use, and I was minded to push-on and explore the magnificent building further."

"But the day was growing late, and I had come upon the sight of the incredible structure after a long and tiring circuit; so, I judiciously resolved to delay my expedition over the intended adventure for the following day, and I returned to the welcome, and the caresses of little Weena."

"But the next morning, I perceived lucidly enough that my curiosity regarding the incomparable 'Palace of Green Porcelain' was a piece of self-deception, which enabled me to shirk, by another day, a necessary experience I dreaded to perform. I promised my soul that I would make the required investigation without further waste of time, and I started-out in the early morning towards a well near the then-familiar ruins of granite and aluminum, my mind determined to accomplish my strategic mission of successfully retrieving my indispensable Time Machine."

"Little Weena ran with me, fearing that I would abandon her. She danced beside me all the way to the well, but when my female companion noticed me leaning over the mouth and looking downward, she seemed strangely disconcerted. 'Good-bye, little Weena,' I said, kissing her on the forehead; and then putting her down, I began to feel over the parapet for the aforementioned climbing hooks. Rather hastily, I may as well confess, for I feared my courage might leak away! At first, Weena watched my descent in sheer amazement. Then, my Eloi lady friend gave a most piteous cry, and running to me, she began to pull and tug at my shoulders with her fragile little hands."

"I think her opposition temporarily unnerved me, but after taking a deep breath, her desperate effort prompted me to proceed downward. I shook her off, perhaps a little too roughly, and in another confusing moment, my feet were deeper inside the throat of the well. I saw Weena's agonized face over the parapet, as she instinctively shrieked and wept, and I smiled to reassure her. Then, I had to look-down at the unstable hooks to which I tightly clung."

"I estimated that I had to clamber-down a vertical shaft of perhaps two-hundred-yards. My descent was aided by means of metallic bars projecting from the sides of the well, and I reckoned that those rungs had been adapted to the needs of a creature, such as a Morlock, much smaller and lighter than myself. However, I was wholly cramped inside the narrow tube, and was soon fatigued by the arduous downward clamber."

"And not simply fatigued! One of the bars had suddenly bent under my weight, and almost swung me off, falling into the blackness beneath. For a moment, I hung dangling by one hand, and after that traumatic experience, I did not dare to rest again during my crucial reconnaissance mission. Though my arms and back were acutely aching, I stubbornly went-on, clambering-down the sheer descent with as quick a motion as possible."

"Glancing upward, I viewed the well's aperture, and observed a small blue disc, in which a star was visible, while little Weena's tiny head showed as a round, black projection. The thudding, piston-like sound of a machine below grew louder and more oppressive to my auditory perception. Everything save that little disc visible above was profoundly dark, and when I again reflexively glanced-up, Weena had disappeared, apparently forgetting all about her new-found companion."

"I was in an agony of discomfort. I had some cowardly thought of trying to go up the shaft again, and leave the cryptic Underworld alone. But even while I turned that craven notion over in my mind, out of obstinate persistence, I continued to descend. At last, with intense relief, I saw dimly coming-up, a foot or so to my right, a slender loophole hollowed-out inside the rock wall. Swinging myself inside the narrow cavity, I found that the opening was the beginning of a tight horizontal tunnel in which I could lie-down and rest. It was not too soon for me to take a breather from my grueling enterprise. My arms hurt; my back was cramped, and my entire body was trembling with the prolonged terror of suffering a fatal fall. Besides those disturbing and distressful factors, the unbroken darkness had had a detrimental effect upon my eyes. All throughout my one-man commando invasion, the rarified and dusty subterranean air was full of the throb and hum of machinery pumping vital oxygen down the shaft. At that juncture, I absolutely believed that my life was in serious jeopardy."

"I do not know how long I was horizontally motionless. In an instant, I was surprised and aroused by a soft hand touching my exposed face. Starting-up in the darkness, I snatched at my matches and, hastily striking one from my dwindling supply, I saw three stooping white creatures, similar to the one I had confronted above ground inside the aluminum ruin, their forms hastily retreating before the flashing light."

"Living as the stinking monsters did, in what appeared to me impenetrable darkness, their frightening red eyes were abnormally large and sensitive, just as are the pupils of the abysmal cave fishes, and their asshole peepers reflected the light in the exact same manner."

"I have no doubt that the encroaching Morlocks could see me in that narrow, rayless obscurity, and that the sickening offenders did not seem to have any fear of me apart from the light that my match had produced. But, as soon as I struck another match in order to again see their location, the fearful fucks, apparently scared of fire, fled *incontinently,* possibly shitting their underwear, and swiftly vanished into dark gutters and tunnels, from which their dazzling red eyes glared at me in the strangest fashion. But with each successive match that had been lit, the Morlocks feared fire less, and advanced more boldly in my direction."

"I tried calling to them in order to receive an answer, but the language, if indeed they possessed speech, was apparently different from that of the Overworld Eloi nincompoops; so as a result, I was left to implementing my own unaided efforts inside enemy territory, and the thought of flight-before-exploration was then even more prevalent inside my disarrayed mind."

"But I stubbornly thought to myself, 'You are really in for it now,' and, feeling my way along the dark alien tunnel, I found the noise of rudimentary machinery growing louder. Presently, the walls fell away from me, and I had entered into a large open space, and striking another dependable match, I realized that I had ventured-inside a vast arched cavern, which stretched into utter darkness beyond the range of my limited light. The view I had of that shadowy central vista was as much as one could observe in the burning of a single match."

"Necessarily, my memory is vague, and virtually inverted. Great shapes like colossal machines rose-out of the immense dimness, and the huge equipment cast grotesque black shadows, in which dim, spectral Morlocks sheltered from the match's bright glare. The dismal place, was very stuffy and noxiously oppressive, and besides those upsetting aspects, the faint odor of freshly-shed blood was evident throughout the musty air."

"Some way down that central rock corridor was a little table of white metal, laden with what seemed a meal. The parasitic Morlocks, at any rate, were exclusively carnivorous! Even at that perilous time, I remember wondering what large animal could have survived to furnish the red meaty joint I saw. It was all very indistinct: the heavy industrial smell; the big unmeaning shapes; the bewildering obscene figures lurking in the bleak shadows, and only waiting for the darkness to aggressively launch a major assault at me again! Then, the essential match burned-down; stung and singed my fingers, and fell from my grip, a wriggling red spot flaring-out in the utter blackness."

"I have since thought how particularly ill-equipped I had been to ever initiate such an invasive experience against a subterranean enemy. When I had started with the Time Machine, I had begun with the absurd assumption that the peaceful men of the Future would certainly be infinitely ahead of ourselves in all their myriad appliances. I had come without arms, without medicine, without anything to smoke; at times, I missed tobacco frightfully! I had arrived in that horrible future setting, even without enough matches to ward-off the primitive Morlocks. If only I had thought of a Kodak! With my camera, I could have flashed that glimpse of the Underworld in a second, and examined it with you gentlemen at leisure. But, as it was, I stood there with only the weapons and the powers that Nature had endowed me with: hands, fists, knuckles, feet, and teeth; these, and four safety-matches that still remained in my possession."

"I was afraid to push my way farther in amongst all that indiscernible machinery in the dark, and it was only with my last glimpse of light I discovered that my store of matches was running terribly low. It had never occurred to me until that moment that there was any need to economize their' usage, and I had ignorantly wasted almost half the box's supply in astonishing the low-intelligence Over-worlders, to whom fire was a novelty. Now, as I say, I had four left, and while I stood in the dismal darkness, a disgusting furry hand touched mine; lank fingers came feeling over my face, and I was once more sensible of smelling a peculiar, unpleasant odor."

"I fancied that I heard the breathing of a crowd of those dreadful little demons swarming like agitated wasps about me. I felt the box of matches in my hand being gently disengaged, and other hands behind me plucking at my loose clothing. The sense of these unseen, very dangerous creatures examining me was indescribably unpleasant. The sudden realization of my total ignorance of their ways of thinking and methods of doing came home to me very vividly in that horrendous, foreboding darkness."

"I vociferously shouted at the furry villains as loudly as my throat could yell. The scumbags started away, and then I could feel the vipers anxiously approaching me again. The human rats clutched at my clothing more boldly, whispering and cooing odd sounds to each other. I shivered violently, and unsuccessfully shouted again, rather discordantly."

"This time the aggressive assailers were not so seriously alarmed, and the shit-heads made queer laughing noises as the determined fucks came back at me. I will confess, gentlemen, that at that crucial interaction, I was excessively frightened. I determined to strike another match and miraculously escape under the protection of its glare. I did so, and eking-out the dim flicker with a scrap of paper taken from my pocket, I made good my retreat to the previously-described narrow tunnel. But I had scarce entered that smaller rock passageway when my light expired, and in the pitch blackness, I could hear the stimulated Morlocks rustling like wind among leaves, and pattering like the rain, as the dastardly, emboldened assholes hurried and scurried after me."

"In a moment of travail, I was clutched by several grimy hands, and there was no mistaking that the reprehensible bastards were trying to haul me back into their sinister domain. I struck another light, and waved its weak flame into their dazzled faces. You can scarce imagine how nauseatingly inhuman the hellish freaks looked, having those pale, chinless faces, and those enlarged, lidless, pinkish-grey eyes, as the fanatical miscreants stared menacingly in their blindness and bewilderment."

"But I did not stay to look or further evaluate my dilemma, this I promise you. I retreated again, and when my second match had extinguished, I struck my third. It had almost burned through when I finally reached the subterranean opening into the vertical shaft. Exhausted, I lay-down upon the edge, for the throb of the great pump below made me giddy."

"Then, I gathered sufficient gumption and felt sideways for the projecting hooks, and, as I did so, my feet were violently grasped from behind, and I was strenuously tugged backward. I managed to light my last match, and it being a dud, instantly extinguished itself. But I had my strong right hand gripped upon a climbing bar, and, kicking for my endangered life, I disengaged myself from the clutches of the frenetically grasping Morlocks, and was soon speedily clambering-up the narrow shaft, while the malignant knaves stayed peering and blinking-up at my ascent; their grotesque eyes seeming like red flashing lights. However, one little wretch followed my clamber for some way, and managed to secure my right shoe as a trophy."

"That climb to safety seemed interminable to me. With the last twenty or thirty feet, a deadly nausea followed by regurgitation occurred. I had the greatest difficulty in keeping my hold the last ten yards of the perilous climb."

"The last few steps were a frightful struggle against the sensation of imminent fainting I had felt. Several times, my head swam in a dizzying whirlpool, and I felt like again barfing-out my guts. At last, however, I somehow deposited my frame over the well-mouth, and stunned and virtually exhausted, I staggered-out of the ruin and stumbled into the blinding sunlight, where I ineptly fell upon my face. Even the common soil smelled sweet and clean. Then, I remember Weena kissing my hands and ears, and I discerned the high-pitched voices of others among the dumb-shit Eloi. Then, for a time, I collapsed and lapsed into deep unconsciousness."

Jay Dubya

Chapter 9

"WHEN NIGHT CAME"

"Now indeed, gentlemen. I seemed to be enveloped in a worst-case-scenario than I had ever before confronted. Hitherto, except during my night's anguish at the loss of the Time Machine, I had felt a sustaining hope of ultimate escape, but that wish was staggered by these new life-threatening discoveries. Before I knew about the fucked-up Morlocks, I had merely thought myself impeded by the childish simplicity of the Eloi, and by some unknown mild forces which I had only to understand in order to overcome; but there was an altogether new element in the nauseous quality of the Morlocks; something inhuman and totally malignant. Instinctively, I loathed their' smelly asses. Before I had ever interacted with their underground repugnance, I had felt as a befuddled man might feel who had accidentally fallen into a deep pit: my concern was with the pit and how to climb-out of it. Now, I felt like a beast snared in a trap, whose vicious enemy would come upon him sooner than later. One thing was certain, and virtually guaranteed: the repulsive Morlocks were no longer remote phantom apparitions. I had plausibly determined that the vile human rats were now my bitter enemies."

"But the opponent which I dreaded most may surprise you. It was the darkness of the New Moon. Little Weena had put this impression into my head by some incomprehensible remarks about the 'Dark Nights'. It was not now such a very difficult problem to guess what the coming Dark Nights might actually signify. The moon was on the wane: in translation, each evening there was a longer interval of greater darkness."

"And I then understood to some slight degree, at least, the reason of the basic fear of the little Upperworld people for the night. I wondered vaguely what foul villainy it might be that the carnivorous

Morlocks performed under the New Moon. I felt pretty sure now that my second hypothesis was all wrong. The Upperworld people might once have been the favored Aristocracy, and the Morlocks their mechanical Proletarian Servants: but that economic relationship had long since passed-away into complete oblivion. The two species that had resulted from the evolution of man were sliding downward towards, or had already arrived at, an altogether new connection. The Eloi, like the Carlovignan kings, had decayed into a mere beautiful futility. The incapacitated numbskulls still possessed the earth on sufferance: since the Morlocks, living a subterranean existence for innumerable generations, had pathetically come at last to find the daylit surface intolerable."

"And I presumed that the villainous Morlocks still made the Eloi's garments out of force of habit, I inferred, and maintained the former Aristocracy in their habitual needs, perhaps through the survival of an old habit of valet service. The furry scumbags performed those practices as a standing horse paws the ground with its foot, or as a man enjoys killing animals in recreational sport: because ancient and departed necessities had impressed the continuation of the habits upon the organism."

"But clearly, the crumbling old order was already in part reversed. The Nemesis of the delicate 'Little Albinos' was gradually creeping-on and literally 'devouring' their remaining culture. Ages ago, thousands of generations ago, man had thrust his brother man out of the ease and the sunshine, and had sentenced the exploited factory workers underground. And now, that punished and exploited brother was coming back, lethally changed into the vile and toxic Morlocks!"

"Already, the victimized Eloi had begun to learn one old-but-reliable lesson anew. The stupid, little assholes were gradually becoming reacquainted with Fear. And suddenly, there came into my memory the recollection of the red meat I had seen lying upon that foreboding Underworld Table. It seemed odd how the recall floated into my already-addled mind: not-stirred-up and agitated, as it were, by the current of my random meditations, but coming in almost like a tremendous tsunami from outside. I tried to recall the exact form and characteristics of it. I had a vague sense of something familiar, like a butcher shop table, but because of my prior cultural civility, I could not cognitively relate *that* deplorable detail with the Eloi's assumed fate at that particular time."

"Still, however, as helpless as the little people were amidst the presence of their then-comprehensible Fear, coming from a more competitive age, I was differently constituted. I came-out of this rivalry-based 1899 dog-eat-dog era of *ours,* this ripe, prime pinnacle of the superior human race, when Fear does not paralyze our deportment, and when mystery has lost its implicit terrors as had existed with prehistoric Neanderthals and Cro-Magnons."

"I, at least, would defend myself to the hilt. Without further delay, I determined to make myself some weapons and find a safe area where I might sleep. With *that* refuge as a base of operation, I could more adequately face this convoluted new world with some semblance of *that* confidence which I had lost in realizing the impending danger of the ever-toxic Morlocks. I felt like I could never soundly sleep again until my slumber was secure from their nightly threat. I shuddered with horror to think exactly how the ugly, vulgar, sordid fucks must already have examined me in my previous sleeps."

"I wondered and wandered during the following afternoon along the valley of the Thames, but found no special location that commended itself to my mind as inaccessible to the contemptible Morlocks. All the high buildings and trees seemed easily available to such dexterous and experienced climbers, judging by their steep, vertical wells."

"Then, to my keen interpretation, the tall pinnacles of the Palace of Green Porcelain and the polished gleam of its attractive facade came back into my memory; and in the evening, taking and transporting Weena like a child upon my shoulders, I ventured hiking-up several hills towards the south-west. The distance, I had erroneously reckoned, was seven or eight miles, but it must have been nearer eighteen. I recalled that I had first seen the place on a moist afternoon, when distances are deceptively diminished."

"In addition, the heel of one of my abused shoes had become loose from my encounter with the vile Morlocks inside the well, and a protruding nail was working through the sole; the loafers were my favorite comfortable old shoes that I often wore about indoors and inside my laboratory, so, to make a lengthy story short, I was nearly lame. And I fathomed that it was already long past sunset, when my eyes came in sight of the marvelous-in-appearance, lustrous-jade palace, silhouetted against the pale-yellow sky."

"Weena had been hugely delighted when I began carrying her in the vicinity of the White Sphinx, but after a monotonous while, my little companion desired, like a toddler, for me to set her down, and my Eloi friend ambled along by my side, completely unimpressed with the majesty of the majestic Green Palace. My little female disciple occasionally darted-off from either hand to randomly pick flowers as valued souvenirs to deposit inside my pockets, which had always puzzled Weena's mental faculties. But at last, my Eloi lady had concluded that they were eccentric kinds of vases, specifically designed for colorful floral decoration. At least Weena's limited thinking had utilized my shirt and pants pockets for *that* unique purpose. And that reminds me! In changing my jacket, I had worn into the future, I found..."

The Time Traveler paused, put his hand into his pocket, and silently placed two withered flowers of an unknown species, rather similar to large white mallows, upon the little table. Then our inimitable host resumed his narrative.

"As the hush of evening crept over the future world, we proceeded over the hill-crest towards Wimbledon, where tennis tournaments had been completely forgotten. Weena grew tired and wanted to return to the familiar dormitory house of grey stone. But I smiled and pointed-out to her the distant pinnacles of the resplendent Palace of Green Porcelain, and I contrived to make her understand that we were seeking safe refuge there that would alleviate her mounting Fear. Now gentlemen, you know that great pause that comes upon the atmosphere influencing the appearance of things just before dusk? Even the breeze stops its gentle movement inside the myriad deciduous and coniferous trees. To be anywhere at twilight, there is always an air of expectation about *that* eerie evening stillness."

"The sky was clear, remote, and cloudless, save for a few horizontal bars showing far down in the sunset. Well, that night, the expectation took and revealed the defined color of my fears. In that darkish calm, my then keen senses seemed preternaturally sharpened. I fancied I could even feel the hollowness of the encroaching evil, existing in condemned ground beneath my feet: my senses could, indeed, almost feeling through the turf the Morlocks active upon their separate ant-hills, meandering hither and thither like a colony of on-a-mission ants, and the nauseating scoundrels impatiently waiting for the surface dark to replace the landscape's light. In my excitement, I fancied that the enemy would receive my invasion of their burrows as a certain declaration of war. And why had the ugly fuck-heads taken my cherished Time Machine?"

"So, accompanied by scared-to-death Weena, we ambled ahead in the quiet suspense, and soon the twilight deepened into night. The clear blue of the distance faded, and one star after another came-out and twinkled. The ground grew dim, and the trees in the vicinity became black outlines. Weena's mounting fears and her increasing fatigue steadily grew upon her. I took her in my arms, and calmly talked and caressed her."

"Then, as the darkness grew deeper and seemingly more-overwhelming, being beleaguered, my Eloi companion put her arms round my neck, and, closing her eyes tightly, pressed her immaculate face against my shoulder."

"So, we cautiously descended a long slope into a shallow valley, and there in the dimness, I almost stumbled into a silent, little river. I carefully waded across, and carrying exhausted Weena, went-up the opposite side of the valley, and trekked past a number of Eloi sleeping houses. And I remember passing by a statue, a sort of Faun replica, or some such past and extinct animal, *minus* the head. Here too were acacias, situated among other indigenous-but-alien shrubs. So far, I had seen nothing of the conniving Morlocks, but it was yet early into the escalating night terror, and the darker hours, before the old moon rose, were still to come."

"From the brow of the next hill, I observed a thick wooded area, spreading wide, and quite black before me. I hesitated while considering the prospect of being savagely ambushed. I could see no end to the array of tall evergreen trees, either to the right or the left. Feeling tired, my feet and legs, in particular, were very sore, I carefully lowered fragile Weena from my shoulders."

"I halted my trek, and aware of possible attack, sat-down upon the turf. I could no longer see the Palace of Green Porcelain, and I was in doubt of my direction in relation to the magnificent edifice. I looked into the thickness of the wood, and thought of what mendacious evils its blackness might hide. Under that dense tangle of branches, one would be out of sight of the stars."

"I imagined that even if there was no hostile danger lurking inside the small forest, there would still be protruding roots to stumble-over, and the abundant tree-boles to strike against. Needless to emphasize, I was very tired, too, after the variety of challenges that had been provided by that rather-laborious day; so, I decided that I would not face any more impeding debacles, but determined that *we* would pass the night upon the open hill."

"Weena, I was glad to find, was fast asleep. I carefully wrapped her in my jacket, and gingerly sat-down upon the grass to wait for the predictable moonrise. The hillside was quiet and deserted, but from the black of the wood, there came now and then a rather-disturbing stir of living things."

"Above me shone the stars and constellations, for the night was very clear. I felt a certain sense of friendly comfort in their familiar twinkling. All the old zodiac formations had gone from the sky; however, that slow movement which is imperceptible in a hundred human lifetimes, had long since rearranged into vastly unfamiliar star groupings. But the Milky Way Galaxy, it seemed to me, was still the same vague, tattered stream of star-dust as of yore. Southward, as

I judged it, was a very bright red star that was absolutely new to me; it was even more splendid and powerful than our own green Sirius. And amid all those scintillating points of eternal light, one bright planet, Jupiter, I believe, shone kindly and steadily like the face of an old friend."

"Looking at those spectacular stars, and possibly planets, there infinite existence suddenly dwarfed my own troubles, and their eternal light easily transcended all the gravities of terrestrial life. I thought of their unfathomable distance, and of their inevitable, drifting movements out of the unknown past, and next contemplating *their* obscure progression into the unknown future."

"I thought of the great precession of the equinoxes that the Earth's poles obediently ordained. Only forty oscillations had that silent revolution occurred during all the years that I had traversed Mother Time. And during those few polar revolutions, all of the activity, all of the traditions, all of the puny-and-complex organizations, the nations, languages, literatures, aspirations, even the mere memory of Civilized Man as I knew him, had been tumultuously swept out of existence. Instead, as unworthy substitutes, there evolved these frail Eloi humanoids, who had regretfully forgotten their high ancestry, and also the 'White Things' of which I evaded in terror."

"Then, I pensively thought of the Great Fear that previously had existed between the two species, and for the first time, with a sudden shiver, came the clear knowledge of what the meat I had seen in the underworld might actually be. Yet, it was too horrible to fully fathom and comprehend! I looked at little Weena, sleeping beside me; her pure-white face shining under the stars, and forthwith, my awareness dismissed its haunting, sorrowful thought."

"Throughout that long and frightful night, I held my mind off the Morlocks as well as I could, and my interest whiled away the precious time with me trying to fancy I could find signs of the old constellations in the new confusion. The sky kept very clear, except for a hazy cloud or so slowly drifting-by. No doubt, I dozed-off at times. Then, as my vigil wore on, came a faintness in the eastward sky, like the reflection of some colorless fire, and the old moon rose, thin, peaked and white."

"And close behind, and overtaking it, and soon overflowing it, the comfort of dawn arrived; pale at first, and then growing pink and warm. Fortunately, no pernicious Morlocks had approached us. Indeed, during my astute vigilance, I had seen none of the dreaded species upon the ominous hillside that night. And in the confidence of renewed day, it almost seemed to my' perception that my former fear had been both unreasonable and unwarranted. I stood-up and found that my foot, with its loose heel swollen at the ankle, had become painful under the already-aching heel; and so, I reluctantly sat-down again, removed my cumbersome remaining shoe, and angrily flung it away."

"I awakened Weena, and we merrily strolled-down into the wood, now green and pleasant, instead of formerly being black and forbidding. We found some delicious-tasting fruit as breakfast to *break* our *fast*. We soon met others of the dainty Eloi tribe, laughing and dancing in the sunlight as though there was no such thing in nature as the 'night-terrors'. And then, I thought once more of the chopped meat that I had seen in the vague Morlock World. I felt assured now of what it was, and from the bottom of my heart, I pitied this last feeble rill from the great flood of human history."

"Clearly, at some time in the Long-Ago travesty of mortal decadence and cultural decay, the Morlocks' food supply, perhaps because of a severe Economic Depression, had run short. Possibly, the species had lived on underground rats and such available vermin. Even now, man is far less discriminating and exclusive in his food choices than he once was; certainly, far less selective than any monkey ancestor."

"However, natural prejudice against human flesh is no deep-seated instinct. And so, these inhuman furry sons of civilized and moral men prevailed! I tried to look at the entire phenomenon in an objective, scientific spirit. After all, the wholly venomous Morlocks were less human and more remote than our cannibal ancestors of three or four thousand years ago. And the basic intelligence that would have made this state of grotesque developments, to a God-fearing person, an unbearable torment, had fundamentally gone. Why should I even trouble myself about what already had been fixed and permanent? I subjectively concluded that these accessible Eloi were mere fatted cattle, which the ant-like Morlocks fed, preserved, and avariciously preyed-upon, and probably supervised the selective breeding of. And then there was tender Weena, innocently dancing at my side!"

"Next, I tried to mentally shield my sensitive mind from vividly imagining the horror that was encroaching upon me, by regarding the tragic approach as a rigorous punishment of human selfishness. Man had been content to live in ease, and to delight upon the labors and achievements of his fellow-man; he had unscrupulously taken Necessity as his watchword and excuse, and in the fullness of time, Necessity had come home to haunt and exterminate him. However great *their* intellectual degradation, I surmised that the afflicted Eloi had kept too much of the human form not to claim my sympathy, my indulgence, and my loyal allegiance."

"I had, at that momentous time, very fuzzy ideas as to the precise course of action I should pursue. My first instinct was to secure some safe place of refuge, and to make myself such arms of metal or stone as I could imaginatively contrive. That necessity was both immediate and paramount."

"In the next place, I hoped to procure some means of making fire, so that I should have the weapon of a torch conveniently at hand, for nothing, I knew, would be more efficient and effective against those very lethal Morlocks."

"Then also, I strongly wanted to arrange, or manufacture, some utilitarian contrivance to break-open the pedestal bronze doors under the White Sphinx. I had in mind constructing a primitive battering ram. I had a mental persuasion that if I could enter those doors and carry a blaze of light before me, I should discover the Time Machine and cleverly initiate a viable escape. I could not imagine the hostile Morlocks being strong enough to move the transportation device farther-away into their mysterious underworld realm."

"I had resolved to transport Weena with me to *our* own 1899 Victorian Age. And turning such schemes over in my bewildered mind, I pursued our path towards the spectacular building which my excited fancy had chosen as *our* next temporary dwelling."

Chapter 10

"THE PALACE OF GREEN PORCELAIN"

"I found the Palace of Green Porcelain, which in its original shape, would have in 1899 been an iconic edifice. When Weena and I approached the structure, around what I suspected had been noon, it was deserted, and like the other massive buildings, had been falling into ruin. Only ragged vestiges of glass remained in its shattered windows, and great sheets of the jade-green facing had deteriorated and fallen-away from the extremely corroded, metallic framework. The sophisticated original architecture had been constructed very high upon a turfy down, and looking north-eastward, before *we* had entered it, I was surprised to have noticed a large estuary, or even an expansive creek, where I judged Wandsworth and Battersea must once have been. I pensively thought then, though I never followed-up the consideration, of what might have happened, or might be happening, to the living animals, and other organisms in the various seas."

"The material of the Palace proved on examination to indeed be porcelain, and along the face of the entrance, I attempted reading a message inscribed in some unknown character. I thought, rather foolishly, that Weena might help me to interpret that obscure vernacular, but I only discerned from her facial expression that the bare idea of writing had never entered her vacuous cranium. My affectionate companion always seemed to me, I had fancied, more human than she really was, perhaps because her very childish mannerisms and her dainty physique were so simplistically human."

"Within the big valves of the entry door, which were half-collapsed and broken, we found, instead of the customary wide hall, a long gallery lit by many side windows. At first glance, I was reminded of a large museum. The tiled floor was thick with dust, and a remarkable array of miscellaneous objects had been superficially shrouded in the same grey covering."

"Then, I perceived, standing strange and gaunt in the center of the vast hall, what was clearly the lower part of a huge skeleton. I recognized by the oblique feet that it was some extinct creature, after the fashion of the prehistoric Megatherium dinosaur family. The enormous skull and the upper bones lay beside it, all coated in the surrounding thick dust, and in one place, where rain-water had dropped through a leak in the roof, parts of the gross-looking exhibit itself had been worn away."

"Further into the straight gallery, I recognized the enormous skeleton barrel of a vegetation-eating Brontosaurus. My original museum hypothesis was quickly confirmed. Going towards the left side, I found what appeared to be sloping shelves, and clearing-away the accumulated thick dust, my eyes discovered the old familiar glass cases indicative of *our* own time. But the display panels must have been air-tight, to accurately judge from the fair preservation of some of their intact contents."

"Clearly to my memory, Weena and I stood among the ruins of some latter-day South Kensington artifacts! Here, apparently, was the Paleontological Section, and a very splendid array of fossils, it certainly must have once been. Obviously, the inevitable processes of decay had been staved off for a time, but with the probable scientific extinction of bacteria and fungi, nature had lost ninety-nine hundredths of its destructive force."

"Here and there, I found traces of the little people in the shape of rare fossils and skeletal remains, their thin bones broken to pieces, or cannibalistically threaded in strings upon flexible reeds. And the exhibition showcases had in some instances been bodily removed, I suspected by the asinine Morlocks, as I had judged. The entire interior of the Green Palace was very eerily silent. The thick dust deadened our extremely-deliberate footsteps. Weena, who had been nonchalantly rolling a sea urchin down the sloping glass of a cracked case, presently came to my side, as I stared about to my right, and very quietly took my hand, and seeking security, dependently stood beside me."

"And at first evaluation, I was so much surprised by this ancient monument of an advanced intellectual age that I gave no thought to the remarkable possibilities and general knowledge it presented. Even my preoccupation about the Time Machine had receded a little from my confounded mind."

"To judge from the size of the immense building, the Palace of Green Porcelain had a great deal more in it than a Gallery of Paleontology; possibly containing a plethora of historical and natural history galleries; it might contain, even a consummate historical library! To me, at least in my present circumstance, such significant book discoveries would be vastly more interesting than this spectacle of old-time geology, wretchedly represented in degenerative decay."

"Exploring further into the vast interior, I found another short gallery running transversely to the first. This smaller corridor appeared to be exclusively devoted to minerals, and the sight of a block of sulfur set my mind running on me producing gunpowder. But I could find no saltpeter; indeed, no usable nitrates of any kind. Doubtless, those 1899 compounds had become obsolete ages ago. Yet the concept of employing sulfur to combat the Morlocks hung heavily in my mind, and the notion set-up a train of thinking I could not resist contemplating."

"As for the rest of the contents of that intriguing gallery, although on the whole, the exhibits were the best preserved of all I had witnessed, I had little interest. I am no specialist in mineralogy, and I proceeded on down a very ruinous aisle running parallel to the first hall I had entered. Quite apparently, this section had been devoted to Natural History, but everything observable had long since passed out of visual recognition. A few shriveled and blackened vestiges of what had once been stuffed carnivorous animals, along with certain mummies' organs, once preserved in jars, and an indiscernible brown form fallen into thick floor dust, the object presumable the remnants of some long-departed gigantic, jungle plant: that was all!"

"Then our cursory expedition arrived at a fantastic gallery of simply colossal proportions, but singularly ill-lit, with its warped and sloped floor running downward at a slight angle from the end at which we had entered. At measured intervals, white globes hung from the ceiling, many of them cracked and smashed, which suggested that originally, the mammoth place had been artificially lit."

"In that new environment, I was more in my element, for rising on either side of me were the huge hulks of complex machines, all greatly corroded with rust, and many broken-down, but remarkably, some still relatively complete. As you gentlemen are well-aware, I have a certain weakness for mechanisms, and I was inclined to linger among those immense engines and various motors. As for the most part, the unidentifiable objects were both a riddle and a conundrum to my temporary fascination. My natural curiosity was quite puzzled, and I could make-out only the vaguest guesses at to what purposes the colossal machines had been used. I fancied that if I could solve their' intricate designs, I should find myself in possession of powers that might be of use against the heinous Morlocks. However, I had no time to assess *their* unknown functionality."

"Suddenly, Weena moved very close to my side. So suddenly that her quick appearance had startled me. Had it not been for her striding forth, I do not think I should have noticed that the floor of the diagonal gallery sloped downward at all. The end I had come in at was quite above ground, and was lit by rare slit-like windows. As we had traversed farther down the full length, the ground and floors came-up against those ramshackle windows, until at last, there was a shallow pit, like the excavated cellar 'area' of a demolished London home, and only a narrow line of daylight shone at the top."

"I advanced slowly along, holding Weena's tender hand, contemplating about the complicated machines, and my curiosity had been too intent upon studying them to notice the gradual diminution of the outside light, until Weena's increasing apprehensions drew my attention to the potentially dangerous situation. Then, I saw that the gallery slanted-down at last into a thick darkness. I hesitated, and then, as I defensively searched around me, my pupils saw that the accumulated dust was less abundant, and the tiled floor's surface less even. Further away towards the dimness, the exhibited sites appeared to be broken by a number of small narrow footprints."

"My sense of the immediate presence of the loathsome Morlocks revived at that sobering comprehension. I felt that I was wasting my time academically exploring the examination of idle and useless machinery. I called to mind that it was already far advanced in the afternoon, and that I still had no weapon, no refuge, and no means of igniting a fire at my disposal. And then, down in the remote blackness of the obscure gallery, my alert ears detected a peculiar pattering, and also the same odd noises I had distinctly heard down the well."

"I immediately took Weena's hand. Then, motivated with a sudden idea, I left her and turned to a machine from which projected a lever not unlike those found extending from a railroad signal-box. Clambering upon the stand, and grasping that desired lever in my hands, I put all my weight upon it sideways. Suddenly, Weena, deserted in the central aisle, began whimpering. I had judged the strength of the lever pretty correctly, for it snapped after a minute's strain, and I rejoined my Eloi young woman with a mace in my hand, more than sufficient, I judged, to crack-open any Morlock skull I might encounter."

"And quite truthfully, I longed very much to kill several Morlocks or so. Very inhuman, you may think, to want to go slaughtering one's own descendants! But it was impossible, somehow, to feel any decent humanity toward the horrendous creatures. Only my disinclination to leave Weena, and a persuasion that if I began to slake my thirst for committing rampant murders, my Time Machine might suffer punitive destruction, and those noteworthy ideas had effectively restrained me from going straight down the gallery and massacring the grunting brutes I heard skittering around."

"Well, with my mighty mace in one hand, and Weena in the other, I exited out of that gallery and into another and still larger one, which at first glance, reminded me of a military chapel that had been hung with tattered flags. The brown and charred rags had been suspended from the side walls, and I presently recognized the decaying vestiges of disintegrated books. The volumes had long since dropped to pieces, and every semblance of print had left their flimsy pages."

"But here and there were warped boards and cracked metallic clasps that told the evolutionary tale well enough. Had I been a scholarly literary professor, I might, perhaps, have moralized upon the futility of all human ambition. But as it was, the thing that struck me with keenest force was the extensive waste of labor to which this somber wilderness of rotting paper testified. At the time, I will confess that I thought chiefly of the *Philosophical Transactions,* and of my own now-meaningless seventeen published papers I had authored upon the subject of physical optics."

"Then, going up a broad, rickety staircase, we came to what may once have been a gallery of technical chemistry. And here I had little hope of making any useful discoveries. Except at one end, where the roof had partially collapsed, this gallery was remarkably well-preserved. I stepped eagerly inside the chamber to investigate every unbroken case. And at last, in one of the really air-tight displays, I found a box of well-preserved matches. Very eagerly I tried lighting one. I was thrilled to learn that the excellent items were perfectly good, and not one iota damp. I turned to Weena. 'Dance!' I hysterically cried in her own tongue. For now, I had a suitable weapon to use against the horrible ape-like creatures we both feared."

"And so, inside that derelict and decrepit green-façade museum, upon the thick soft carpeting of dust, to Weena's huge delight, I solemnly performed a kind of composite dance, whistling *The Land of the Leal* as cheerfully as I could, while hoarsely singing in a raspy baritone. In part, my gyrating performance was a modest *cancan;* in part a step dance; in part a skirt dance, as far as my tail-coat permitted, and in part an original polka execution. For, quite frankly, I am naturally inventive, as you gentlemen well-know."

"Now, I still think that for this box of matches to have escaped the wear of time for immemorial years was a most extraordinary revelation, and as for me personally, their' viable existence was a most fortunate discovery. Yet, oddly enough, I found a far unlikelier substance, and that chemical compound was camphor. It had been contained in an air-tight jar, that by chance, I suppose, had been expertly hermetically sealed. I fancied, at first analysis, that the material had been paraffin wax, and I demonstrably smashed the glass accordingly. But the nasty, potent odor of camphor was unmistakable. In the universal decay that centuries had applied, that volatile substance had chanced to survive, perhaps through many thousands of passing years."

"I was about to throw the camphor jar away, but I remembered from a university chemistry seminar that the substance was flammable, and would burn with a good bright flame; and was, in fact, quite capable of providing me with an excellent candle. So, I squeezed and stored the tight jar inside my pants pocket among the fragrant flowers that Weena had stuffed. However, I found no explosives in that intriguing gallery, nor any means of breaking-down the White Sphinx's solid bronze doors. As yet, my iron crowbar was the most helpful tool that my frantic search had chanced upon. Nevertheless, I left that dismal gallery greatly elated."

"I cannot tell you all the story of that long afternoon. It would require a great effort of memory to recall my curious explorations in all the proper order. I remember a long gallery of rusting stands of arms, and how I hesitated between my crowbar and a hatchet, or an available sword, for I could not carry those objects and also attend to Weena's protection. I rationally reckoned that my iron bar promised the best results against smashing-open the pedestal's sturdy bronze gates."

"There were a number of guns, pistols, and rifles on display, but most were masses of useless rust, but many were of some new yet-known alloy, and still fairly sound. But any cartridges or powder there may once have been on exhibit had already rotted into dust."

"In one corner, in which I searched, were charred and shattered metallic pieces; perhaps shrapnel, I imagined, the genesis of which had possibly been an explosion among the multitude of specimens. In another place was a vast array of statues and idols: Polynesian, Mexican, Grecian, Phoenician, Egyptian, and virtually every country on Earth, I should think. And here, yielding to an irresistible impulse, I scribbled my full name upon the nose of a dust-laden demonic monster, from South America, I believe, that particularly captured my intellectual fancy."

"As the evening drew onward, my interest in academic matters conversely waned. Weena and I trudged through gallery after gallery, dusty, silent, often ruinous; the many exhibits sometimes being mere heaps of rust and lignite, and sometimes a bit fresher in general appearance. In one place, I suddenly found myself near the model of a tin mine, and then by the merest accident, I discovered, in an air-tight case, two dynamite cartridges! I boisterously shouted 'Eureka!' in revered imitation of Archimedes, and using my iron club, smashed-open the case with joy. Next came a serious doubt. I hesitated. Then, selecting a little side gallery, I made my dynamite idea an experiment. I never felt such a disappointment as I did in waiting five, ten, fifteen-minutes for an explosion that never occurred. Of course, the sticks were dummies, as I might have guessed from their aged presence. In retrospect, I really believe that had the dynamite sticks not been usable, I should have rushed-off and foolishly blown-up the White Sphinx, the pedestal, the bronze doors, and finally and accidentally, the Time Machine, into certain non-existence."

"It was after that sobering episode, I think, that we came to a little open court within the central Green Palace aisle. It was turfed, and had three bearing fruit-trees growing inside. So, we rested and refreshed ourselves with sugared sustenance. Towards sunset, I began to consider our current position. Night was creeping upon us, and my desired inaccessible hiding-place had still to be found. But that troubled me very little now. I had in my possession a thing that was, perhaps, the best of all defenses against the reprehensible

Morlocks. I had matches! I had the ignitable camphor inside my pants pocket, too, if an emergency blaze would be needed."

"Although dusk was rapidly approaching, it soon dawned upon me that the best strategy we could exercise would be to pass the night out in the open, protected by the glare of a fire. In the morning, there was the essential re-possession of my escape mechanism, the indispensable Time Machine. To accomplish that goal, as yet, I had only my iron mace. But now, with my growing knowledge of my general environment, I felt very differently towards those rusty bronze doors. Up to that time, I had refrained from violently forcing the obstacles open, largely because of the mysteries that eerily existed on the other side. Both the locked doors and the fucked-up Morlocks had never impressed me as either being very strong, and I hoped to use my iron bar to adequately achieve my planned departure from that most-disturbing future, chaotic bronze pedestal environment. My military campaign against my dreaded, furry enemies was about to commence.

Jay Dubya

Chapter 11

"IN THE DARKNESS"

"All the while, I felt like a hypocritical iconoclast, attempting to objectively explore the future, and then become rich and famous, only to discover that my well-intended journey had become fraught with delusion, failure, and frustration. Weena and I emerged through the majorly damaged Green Palace doors while the sun was still in part above the horizon. I was determined to surely reach the White Sphinx early the next morning, and so, I purposely pushed through the woods that had stopped me on the previous journey to the vast decrepit museum. My plan was to pace as far ahead as possible that night, and then, building a suitable fire, to sleep in the protection of its glare."

"Accordingly, as we trekked along, I gathered any large sticks or dried grass I could amass, and presently had my arms full of such litter. Thus loaded, our progress was slower than I had anticipated, and besides, Weena's energy was quickly spent from hiking. And also, I began suffering from drowsiness, too; so that it was full night before we eventually reached the designated woods."

"Upon the shrubby hill of its edge, Weena would have stopped, fearing the great darkness before us; but a singular sense of impending calamity, that should indeed have served me as a significant warning, drove me onward. I had been without sleep for a night and two full days, and I was feverish and fairly irritable. I felt sleep coming upon me, and the detestable Morlocks with it."

"While we hesitated, among the black bushes behind us, and dim against their blackness, I spotted three crouching figures. My mind considered the horrible possibility that before Weena might be captured, killed, and malignantly butchered, the perverted Morlocks, being partially human, might lustfully and animalistically attempt raping my tiny Eloi sweetheart, and sexually assaulting and molesting my petite lady friend. Those disgusting considerations I found to be morally abominable!"

"There was low scrub and long grass all about us, and I did not feel safe from the human rodents' insidious approach. The small forest, I calculated, was rather less than a mile across. If we could get through the thickets to the bare hillside, there, as it seemed to my scrutiny, was an altogether safer resting-place to camp; I thought that with my matches and my camphor, I could contrive to keep my path illuminated through the woods' interior."

"Yet, it was plainly evident that if I were to flourish matches with my hands, I should have to abandon my firewood; so, rather reluctantly, using discretion, I put-down the heap. And then, it came into my head that I would amaze and entertain our itinerant Morlock spies behind our route by cunningly lighting the dry branches. I was to discover the atrocious folly of this frivolous proceeding, but at the time, it came to my mind as an ingenious move for covering our retreat and also, effectively distracting our nefarious enemies."

"Now gentlemen, I don't know if you've ever thought what a rare thing flame and corresponding fire must be in the absence of modern man in a very dry temperate climate. The sun's heat is rarely strong enough to burn the skin, even when it is focused by dewdrops, as is sometimes the case in more tropical countries. Lightning may blast and blacken, but it rarely gives rise to widespread fire. Decaying vegetation may occasionally smolder with the heat of its fermentation, but that phenomenon hardly ever results in producing flame. In this totally insane Morlock-Eloi decadence, too, the art of fire-making, along with any knowledge of the mythological Titan, Prometheus, had been forgotten on the Earth. The red tongues that went licking-up my ignited heap of wood were an altogether new and strange experience to Weena."

"Amazingly, my petite girl wanted to run and play with it, believing that the red flares were some novel type of exciting futuristic toy. I believe she would have cast herself into the raging blaze had I not physically restrained her. But I caught her up, and in spite of the little doll's crying and resisting struggle, I, carrying her on my shoulders, plunged boldly into the center of the shadowy forest. For a little way, the glare of my fire had helpfully lit the path. Looking back presently, I could see, through the crowded stems and shrubs, that from my pile of sticks and dried-up leaves, the blaze had spread to some adjacent bushes, and a curved line of flames was creeping-up the hill's grassy crest, causing a spreading conflagration."

"I laughed at that raging fire, with my mind knowing that the Morlocks had no fire departments or special equipment to quell the inferno. I again turned my attention to the dark trees before me. It was very black, and Weena clung to my neck convulsively, but there was still, as my eyes grew accustomed to the darkness, sufficient light for me to avoid the ground stems and the low tree limbs. Up ahead, despite poor visibility, the trail was simply black, except where a gap of remote blue sky shone-down upon us here and there. I halted, but lit none of my matches, because I had no hand free to strike one. At that point, upon my left arm, I carried my little sixty-pound companion, and in my right hand I held my heavy iron bar."

"For some distance, I heard nothing except the crackling twigs under my feet; the faint rustle of the gentle breeze above; my own breathing, and the throb of the enlarged blood-vessels inside my astute ears. Then, I seemed to become aware of a certain pattering behind me. I pushed-on grimly as the continuous pattering grew more distinct, and then my ears caught the same queer sound and voices that I had heard laughing and cooing in the formidable Underworld. There were evidently several of the Morlocks in our midst, and the contemptible, furry fuck-heads were closing in upon us. Indeed, in another minute, I felt a definite tugging at my jacket, and then, something pulling at my left arm. And petite Weena shivered violently in reaction to the ambush's accelerating danger, and my companion became quite still out of being petrified from extreme fright."

"It was time to light a match to thwart the loathsome predators' malicious foray. But to get and strike it to light, I must first put Weena down. I did so, and, as I fumbled with my pocket, a wild struggle and scramble began about my knees, and my Eloi friend remained perfectly silent and submissive as the same peculiar cooing sounds emanated from the Morlocks' raspy throats. Soft little filthy hands, too, were creeping over my coat and back, touching even my neck and throat."

"Then fortunately, the dry match scratched and fizzed. I held it flaring and prematurely dying, and saw the white backs of the Morlocks dashing-away in flight amid the black trees. I hastily took a lump of camphor from my pocket, and prepared to light it as soon as the fading match should fully wane. Then, I looked-down at Weena. She was lying upon the turf, clutching my feet and quite motionless, with her dainty face touching the ground."

"With a sudden fright, I stooped to lift her to her feet. She seemed scarcely to breathe. I successfully lit the block of camphor, flung it to the ground, and as it split and flared-up, the fire burst drove-back the intimidated Morlocks into the shadows. I recollect me gently kneeling-down and lifting Weena to an upright position. In the meantime, the entire woods behind us seemed full of the stirring and murmuring of a great company of patrolling Morlocks!"

"Weena, during her delirium panic attack, seemed to have fainted. I placed her carefully upon my shoulder and rose to push-on, and then there came a horrible realization. In maneuvering with my matches and assisting Weena, I had turned myself about several times, and now I had not the faintest idea in what direction lay my path. For all I knew, lacking a compass, I might be facing back towards the Palace of Green Porcelain, instead of heading towards the White Sphinx and the pilfered Time Machine."

"I found myself breathing heavily, with my whole anatomy in a cold sweat. I had to think rapidly as to what to do next. I determined to build a large fire and encamp where we were, out in the open. I put Weena, still motionless, down upon a turfy spot, and very hastily, as my first lump of camphor waned, I began collecting additional sticks and leaves to keep my mini-forest-fire going. Here and there, out of the eerie darkness, all around me, the Morlocks' eyes shone like bright carbuncles."

"The camphor lump flickered and soon went-out. I lit another match, and as I did so, two white forms that had been approaching Weena scooted hastily away. One was so blinded by the light that the dumb-fuck came straight for me, and out of a need for survival, I felt his bones grind under the blows of my fist. The furry asshole gave a whoop of dismay, staggered a little way, and fell-down in excruciating pain. I lit another piece of camphor, and went-on gathering flammable material for my improvised bonfire."

"In my enterprise, I noticed how dry was most of the foliage hanging-down above me, for since my arrival upon the Time Machine, I estimated a matter of a week, no substantial rain had fallen. So, instead of casting about among the trees for fallen twigs, I obsessively began leaping-up and dragging-down accessible branches. Very soon, I had a choking, smoky fire of green wood and dry sticks, and could easily economize my camphor. Then, I turned to where Weena lay beside my iron mace. I tried what I could to revive her from shock, but my little woman lay still like one dead. At that interval, I could not even satisfy myself whether or not she was breathing."

"Now, the smoke of the fire beat over towards me, and it must have made me heavily inhale. Moreover, the vapor of camphor was prevalent throughout the air. My fire would not need replenishing for an hour or so. I felt very weary after my tiresome exertion, and consequently, sat-down."

"The encompassing woods, too, was full of a dull murmur that I did not understand. I seemed just to reflexively nod, and occasionally open my eyes. But all was dark, and the Morlocks again had their soft, stinking hands upon me. Flinging-off their clinging fingers, I hastily felt in my pocket for the match-box, and was stunned to realize that it was gone! Then the hairy bastards gripped and swiftly closed-upon me again. In a moment, I knew what had happened. I had fallen asleep; my fire had gone-out, and the bitterness of death trespassed over my besieged soul."

"The forest suddenly seemed full of the smell of burning wood. I was caught by the neck, by the hair, by the arms, and soon tumultuously pulled-down. It was indescribably traumatic in the darkness, feeling all those soft, stench-laden, belligerent fuck-heads heaped upon me. I felt as if I had been trapped inside a monstrous spider's web. In less than a minute, I was overpowered by their sheer numbers, and plunged-down to the ground."

"I felt little teeth nipping at my neck, and that sensation made me want to vomit. My will had the wherewithal to roll-over, and as I did so, my hand luckily came against my iron lever. That wonderful, tacit identification afforded me immediate strength. Adrenaline rushed through my arteries and veins. I struggled to become erect upon my feet, and crazily shaking the human rats from my back, and, holding the iron bar short, I thrust where I judged their hideous-looking faces might be. I could feel the penetration of flesh and bones under my powerful blows, and for a moment, I was free of their' very persistent onslaught."

"The strange and primeval exultation that so often seems to accompany hard fighting in order to endure came upon me. I knew that both Weena and I were lost without any sense of direction, but I determined to make the Morlocks pay dearly for their meat. I stood with my back to a tree, savagely swinging and thrusting the metal bar before me, not wanting to be a victim to cannibalism. The whole wood was full of the stir and cries of the maniacal, white-furred attackers. My hope of survival was running short."

"A minute of extreme active battle passed. The Morlocks screeching voices seemed to rise to a higher pitch of excitement, and their impetuous movements and awkward punches accelerated even faster. Yet being blinded by the fire, none of their fists came within reach of my chin. I anxiously stood upon the open ground, intensely glaring at the utter blackness."

"Then suddenly, came inspirational hope. What if the Morlocks were afraid? And close on the heels of that conjecture came a rather strange observation. The overhead darkness seemed to gradually grow vaguely luminous. Very dimly, I began to recognize the presence of injured Morlocks lying about my feet; three were badly battered at my left, and then, my taxed brain realized with sudden delight and incredulous surprise, that the others were swiftly running away, in an incessant stream of ape-like bodies through the nearby woods. And their backs seemed no longer white, but rather reddish. As I stood with my mouth agape, I noticed a little red spark go drifting across a gap of starlight between the tree branches, and vanish. And at that visualization, I understood the smell of burning wood, the low murmur that was growing now into a gusty roar; yes, the approaching red glow, and simultaneously, the Morlocks' frenetic flight."

"Stepping-out from behind my tree and looking back towards my enemy's wild retreat, I noticed, through the black pillars of the nearer evergreens, the flames of the still-burning forest. I smiled, realizing that the advancing blaze was actually my first fire coming after me. With that, my emotions changed when I peered-down and looked for comatose Weena, but to my utter disappointment, my Eloi friend was gone."

"The hissing and crackling noises behind me, along with the explosive thud with each fresh tree bursting into flame, left little time for mental reflection. My iron bar still gripped, I followed in the Morlocks' path, hoping to rescue and salvage captured Weena. It was a close and exhaustive race. Once the flames crept forward so swiftly on my right as I sprinted that I was outflanked, and had to pivot-off to the left in order to avoid being incinerated. But at last, I emerged upon a small open space, and as I did so, a shrieking Morlock came blundering towards me, and soon past me, and went straight ahead, leaping directly into the fire in a weird self-sacrifice!"

"And now, I was to see the most peculiar and horrible phenomenon, I think, of all that I beheld in that future age. The whole space around me was as bright as day, saturated with the reflection of the wild forest fire. In the center was a bare, weedless space, surmounted by a scorched hawthorn. Beyond that spectacle was another arm of the burning woods, with yellow tongues already writhing-out from it, completely encircling the entire space with a surging fence of fire."

"Upon the hillside were some thirty-to-forty Morlocks, dazzled by the intense light, and suffering from the tremendous heat. And the blinded throng was blundering hither and thither against each other, wholly confused in their clumsy bewilderment."

"At first, I did not realize their utter futility, and I struck furiously at their heads with my trusty bar, and in a frenzy of heightened fear, as the dumb-ass shit-heads clumsily approached me, I enthusiastically killed one staggering numbskull, and severely crippled several more. But when I had watched the gestures of one of the stupid assholes groping under the scorched hawthorn, and heard the moans of his ailing colleagues, I was assured of their absolute helplessness and misery within the brilliant glare, and adjusting to reality, I struck no more of the furry dirtbags."

"Yet every now and then, one of the carnivorous dipshits would come straight towards me, setting loose a quivering horror that made me quick to elude his incensed charge. At one time, the flames died-down somewhat, and I feared that the bellicose monsters would presently be able to see and attack me. I was thinking of continuing the major fight by killing some more of the rabble before *that* effect should materialize; but the ongoing blaze burst-out again, rather brightly. I relaxed a bit, and rationally stayed my hand. I ambled about the hill among their suffering forms, and discreetly avoided the sub-humans, all the while searching for some trace of sweet Weena. But in truth, little Weena was gone."

"At last, I sat-down upon the summit of a hilltop, my mind being in a lugubrious and dejected state. My blurry eyes watched that strange, incredible company of blind villains groping to-and-fro, and their ugly mouths making uncanny noises to each other, as the glare of the fire beat-upon the enemy's erratic, semi-paralyzed bodies. The coiling uprush of smoke streamed across the sky, and through the rare tatters of that red canopy, remote as though my rivals belonged to another universe, shone the little galaxy stars. Two or three Morlocks came stumbling and blundering into me, and I drove them off with blows of my bloody fists, trembling as I did so."

"For the most part of that terrifying night, I was persuaded that the whole misadventure was a devastating nightmare. I bit my parched tongue and screamed in a passionate desire to escape that horrid setting. I beat the ground with my fists, and got-up and sat-down again, and wandered here and there, and again sat down, dreading and mourning the unknown fate of lost Weena."

"Then, I would fall to rubbing my eyes and calling upon God to let me awake from my unbearable nightmare. Thrice I saw Morlocks put their heads down in a kind of agony, and being both disoriented and attracted, wildly rush into the roaring, escalating flames. But, at last, above the subsiding red of the extensive forest fire; above the streaming masses of billowing black smoke; along with the whitening and blackening tree stumps, and the diminishing numbers of those dim creatures, gratefully came the bright light of dawn."

"I again desperately searched for traces of Weena, but there were none to be found anywhere. It was plainly evident, I concluded, that the fucked-up enemy shit-heads had, out of fright, inadvertently left her poor little body to be cremated somewhere inside the burning forest. I cannot describe how it relieved me to think that her tiny corpse had coincidentally escaped the awful fate to which it seemed destined. As I thought of that prospect, I was almost moved to again begin a wicked massacre of the helpless abominations kneeling about me, but surrendering to rationality, I contained my need for revenge."

"The grassy knoll, as I have described, was a kind of island in the forest. From its crest, I could now distinguish through a haze of smoke the Palace of Green Porcelain, and from *that* familiar sighting, I could obtain my bearings for the White Sphinx. And so, leaving the remnant of those remaining damned souls still awkwardly scampering hither and thither, and incessantly moaning and groaning, as the day became clearer, I tied some soft grass about my feet and limped-on across smoking ashes and black stems that still pulsated internally with occasional embers. My tired legs were slowly ambling towards the suspected hiding-place of the Time Machine."

"In my travel, or should I say 'travail', I walked very deliberately, for I was almost thoroughly fatigued, as well as lame, and I felt an intense wretchedness and personal guilt when contemplating the horrible death of little Weena. Assessing my mounting guilt, the entire incident seemed an overwhelming calamity, all caused by the raging forest fire that I had created."

"Now, gentlemen, in this old comfortable room, it is more like the sorrow of a dream than an actual loss. But that bleak morning, the catastrophic experience left me absolutely melancholy and lonely again; yes, terribly alone. I began to think of this cozy Richmond house of mine, of this warm fireside, of some of you, my Thursday evening dinner friends, and with such nostalgic thoughts, came a strong longing that evolved into great emotional pain."

"But, as I walked over the smoking ashes, under the bright morning sky, I made an encouraging discovery. In my trouser pocket were still some loose, dry matches that I had obtained from the Palace of Green Porcelain. The containing box must have leaked separate matches before it had somehow been lost in the decisive forest fight."

Chapter 12

"THE WHITE SPHINX TRAP"

" **A** bout eight or nine in the morning, I came to the same seat of yellow twisted metal from which I had viewed the world upon the first evening of my arrival. I thought of my hasty conclusions upon that evening, and could not refrain from laughing bitterly at my rambunctious confidence. Here was the same beautiful scene; the same abundant foliage; the same splendid palaces and magnificent ruins, and the same silver river running between its fertile banks. The attractive robes of the beautiful people moved hither and thither amongst the tall trees. Some were bathing in exactly the same place where I had rescued Weena, and that sentimental memory suddenly gave my' heart a keen stab of pain. And like blots upon the landscape rose those sinister cupolas, constructed above the wells leading to the hellish Underworld."

"I thoroughly then understood what all the beauty of the Overworld people covered below. Very pleasant was their sunny day, as pleasant as the daily sunshine of the unassuming cattle grazing in the field. Like the naïve cows in the pasture, the Eloi knew of no enemies, and provided against no needs. And predictably, their doomed end was quite the same."

"I grieved to think how brief the dream of the human intellect had been, and in an instant, *that* aspiration declined and disintegrated into mental oblivion. Somewhere in history, intelligence had committed suicide. Mankind had set itself steadfastly towards comfort and ease, establishing a balanced society with security and permanency as its watchword; civilization had somewhat attained its hopes with the ascension of the Eloi, but only to come to this satanic and grotesque destiny at last."

"Once upon a time, life and property must have reached almost absolute safety. The rich had been assured of their lucrative wealth and comfort, and the subterranean toiler assured of his life and factory work. No doubt in that near-perfect world, there had been no unemployment problem, along with no irritating social question left unsolved. And over the myriad eons, a great quiet had eventually followed."

"It is a law of nature we tend to overlook; that specific rule being the mantra that intellectual versatility is the compensation for change, danger, and trouble. An animal that is perfectly in harmony with its environment is, in actuality, a perfect mechanism. Nature never appeals to intelligence until habit and instinct are diminished to uselessness. There is no intelligence where there is no change, and no need for change. Only those animals partake of intelligence who have to meet, out of necessity, a huge variety of incumbent needs and dangers. Adjusting to dangers is truly the Mother-of-Survival!"

"So, as I perceived it, the Upperworld Aristocracy had drifted towards its feeble prettiness, and the Underworld Proletariats had been assigned to mere underground mechanical industry. But that perfect state had lacked one important factor, even for the implementation of subterranean mechanical perfection: that essential element was absolute permanency."

"Apparently, as time upon the Earth advanced onward, the feeding of an Underworld, however it was achieved, had eventually become disjointed. Mother Necessity, who had been staved off for a few thousand centuries, came back again, and she began exercising her influence below the surface. The Underworld, being in contact with machinery, which, however almost-perfect, still requires some basic thought to maintain, outside of habit; in short, the Lower-World inhabitants had probably retained more initiative to engage in labor, if ostensibly retaining less of every other human character, than the naïve Upperworlders. And when other meat failed their' diets, the ancestors of the Morlocks turned to what old habit and tradition had hitherto forbidden; namely cannibalism. The scarcity of meat led to this queer relationship of the Eloi to the Morlocks. This explains the absence of dogs, cats, horses, cattle and other large mammals, all of which ran-out of existence when those food sources had been slaughtered by the hungry and carnivorous Undergrounders."

"So, I say, gentlemen; that is how I viewed and interpreted my' environment in my last glimpse of the future world of Eight Hundred and Two Thousand, Seven Hundred and One. It may be as wrong an explanation as mortal wit could invent. However, it is how the abysmal living relationship shaped itself to me, and as which I'm accurately reporting my observations to you."

"Now, my good friends, after the fatigues, excitements, and terrors of the past week, and in spite of my tremendous grief, that cherished seat I was occupying atop the aluminum pile, and the tranquil view I was savoring, along with the warm sunlight I was relishing, were all very pleasant and satisfying. I was extremely tired and sleepy, and soon my speculative theorizing passed into necessary dozing. Catching myself at that physical need, I took my own hint, and spreading myself out upon the dry turf, I enjoyed a long and refreshing sleep in the warm sunshine. Unfortunately, I dreamed of poor Weena, and of her unknown fate."

"I awoke a little before the setting sun. I now felt safe against being caught napping by the ruthless Morlocks, and, stretching myself, I strode on down the hill towards the arcane White Sphinx. I had my crowbar in one hand, and the other hand played with the remaining matches inside my pants pocket."

"And now came a most unexpected thing. As I approached the pedestal of the White Sphinx, I soon found that the bronze valves were wide open. The Morlocks evidently had possessed some small degree of cunning, and the uncivilized brutes had unscrupulously and mechanically slid the portals down into grooves."

"At that discovery, I suspiciously stopped short before the opening, sensing a stealthy trap being set, and thus, I hesitated to enter. But I no longer wished to shirk my primary objective of valiantly reclaiming the Time Machine, so I determined to confront whatever wicked scheme that my furry, sneaky opponents had in store."

"Within the pedestal was a small apartment, and upon a raised platform in the right corner was stationed the Time Machine. I still had the small starting levers inside my pocket. So there, in the dim light, after all my elaborate preparations for the careful siege of the White Sphinx, was what I perceived as a meek surrender. I tossed-away my iron bar, almost sorry not to again use it."

"A sudden thought came into my head as I stooped towards and into the low portal. For once, at least, I grasped the mental operations of the moronic Morlocks. Suppressing a strong inclination to laugh, I stepped through the bronze frame, and slowly walked-up to the inimitable Time Machine. I was surprised to find that the apparatus had been carefully oiled and cleaned. I have since suspected that the asshole Morlocks had even partially taken it to pieces, while trying in their dimwit way, to grasp its superb mechanical purpose."

"Now, as I stood and examined my marvelous invention, finding true pleasure in the mere touch of the contrivance, the attack that I had expected suddenly happened. The bronze panels instantaneously slid-up and struck the bronze frame with a jolting clang. I was in the dark, dangerously trapped with no allies. So, that is what the Morlocks erroneously thought. I chuckled gleefully at their fucked-up stupidity."

"I could already hear their zany murmuring, along with their peculiar laughter as the irate brood came-out of a tunnel, wildly charging towards me. Very calmly, I tried striking a match. My simple task was that I only had to fix on the levers and depart the chaotic scene like a fleeting ghost. But I had overlooked one little circumstance. The matches were of that abominable kind that light only when scratched upon the containing box."

"You may imagine how all my calm vanished quicker than a magician's rabbit. The furry demons were close upon me, ready to eliminate me from existence. One of the more-brazen shit-heads boldly touched me. I made a sweeping blow in the dark at his comrades with the dashboard levers, and I frantically endeavored to scramble into the machine's saddle. Then, came one stinking hand latching upon me, and then another. Next, I had simply to fight against their persistent fingers for control of my essential levers, and at the same time, I needed to feel for the studs over which those small handles fitted. The aggressive assholes almost stole away one of the levers from me, which I was using as a brass knuckles' substitute. As the vital object slipped from my hand, I had to butt my attackers in the dark with my hard head. I could hear the Morlocks' skulls ring like empty bells. Their vain attempt at recovering and possessing the operating tool miraculously ended in failure. The whole White Sphinx battle was a nearer physical encounter than the recent fight in the forest. For sure, I was quite fortunate to escape that frenetic last scramble and brawl."

"But at last, the remaining lever had been securely tightened and fixed into position, and soon skillfully pulled-over. The clinging, greasy, grimy hands magically slipped away from my squirming body. The darkness presently fell from my eyes. I found myself magically swirling and whirling in the same artificial grey light and tumult that I have already described."

Jay Dubya

Chapter 13

"THE FUTURE VISION"

"**I** have already told you, gentlemen, of the sickness and confusion that comes with the thrill of time traveling. And that second episode in the saddle, because of my life-or-death conflict with the Morlocks, I was not properly seated, but instead situated sideways, and also in an extremely unstable fashion. For an indefinite time, I clung to the machine for dear life as it swayed, gyrated, and vibrated further into the future. The treasured mechanism, being an inanimate object without a brain, was quite unheeding and unsympathetic as to how I was moving, which was much like an American cowboy riding upon an untamed bucking bronco. And when I brought myself to glance at the dashboard's rotating dials, I was amazed to realize where I and my machine were heading."

"Now, one dial records days; and another thousands of days; another millions of days, and a fourth showing thousands of millions. Then, instead of reversing the levers, I had in my hasty departure from the White Sphinx inadvertently pulled the small handles over, so as to again go forward into time, and when I came to look at those special indicators, I found that the thousands hand had been sweeping around as fast as the seconds hand of a watch, amazingly, in a very rapid manner, even further into the distant future."

"As I speedily drove-on, a peculiar change crept over the appearance of everything I had been witnessing from my awkward vantage point upon the saddle. The palpitating greyness grew darker; although, I was still bounding-about upon my seat, traveling ahead with prodigious velocity."

"The blinking succession of day and night, which was usually indicative of a slower pace, returned, and grew more and more marked as I slowed-down my incomparable means of time transportation. At first, that perpetual alternation puzzled my senses very much. The transitions of night and day gradually grew slower and slower, and so did the passage of the eternal sun across the wan sky, until the flickering seemed to stretch through mere centuries."

"At last, a steady twilight brooded over the Earth; yes, a dusky twilight only broken now and then when a comet glared and streamed across the darkish sky. The band of light that had indicated the sun had long since disappeared; for our nearest star had ceased to set. Earth's glowing companion, the source of our planet's main energy supply, simply rose and fell in the west, and grew ever broader and more-reddish than even in the era of the Eloi and the Morlocks. All traces of the moon had vanished. The circling of the stars, revolving slower and slower, had given place to rather-simple creeping points of light."

"At last, some short time before I determined to stop, the sun, red and very large, halted motionless upon the horizon, showing its form as a vast dome shining with a dull heat, and now and then, suffering a momentary extinction like a flickering candle about to expire. At one time, Old Sol had for a little while glowed more brilliantly again, but it speedily reverted-back to its sullen red heat. I perceived by this slowing-down of the sphere's rising and setting that the work of the tidal drag was finally done."

"Now gentlemen; Mother Earth had come to rest with one side facing the sun, even as in our own time, the moon faces the Earth without ever spinning. Very cautiously, for I remembered my former headlong fall at the base of the White Sphinx, I began to methodically cease my speedy forward motion. Slower and slower went the circling hands until the thousands dial seemed motionless, and its plain reading was no longer a mere mist showing upon its registering indicator. I was still traveling slower, until my eyes noticed the dim outlines of a desolate beach visibly becoming into focus."

"I stopped very gently and vigilantly sat upon the Time Machine, looking around my new environment in absolute wonder. The cloudless sky was no longer blue. North-eastward, the atmosphere was inky black, and out of the blackness shone brightly, and steadily looking upward, my vision perceived the more permanently set pale white stars, sort of still uniquely situated in their conventional places."

"Overhead, the higher stratosphere was a deep Indian red, and quite starless. And south-eastward, the denser atmosphere grew brighter to a glowing scarlet where, cut by the horizon, lay the huge hull of the sun, appearing red and motionless. The rocks about me were of a harsh reddish color, and all the traces of life that I could see at first impression were the intensely slimy-green vegetation and the accompanying dull fungus that covered every projecting point on the south-eastern face. It was the same rich green that one sees upon forest moss, or on the lichen clusters in underground caves: plants which like those particular varieties usually grow in perpetual twilight."

"The Time Machine was stationary, occupying an elevated position upon a sloping beach. The sea stretched away to the south-west, to rise into a sharp bright horizon against the wan sky. There were no breakers or waves, for not a breath of wind was stirring. Only a slight oily swell rose and fell like a gentle breathing, and its activity showed that the eternal sea was still moving and living, but the Thames River was nowhere in sight."

"And along the margin where the water sometimes broke was a thick incrustation of accumulated salt, reflecting the color pink under the lurid sky. There was a sense of extreme oppression tormenting my head's emotions, and I noticed that I was breathing very fast and deep. The overall sensation reminded me of my only experience of mountaineering in the Swiss Alps, and from that, I judged the air to be much more rarefied than it is now in 1899 London."

"Far away up the desolate slope, my ears heard a harsh screech, and my eyes noticed a large flying insect, something akin to a huge white butterfly, and as large as an eagle, go slanting and fluttering-up into the sky, continuously circling in a consistent pattern, and then disappearing over some low hills beyond. The sound of its screeching voice was so dismal that I shivered and seated myself more firmly upon the machine, just in case I needed to evacuate in a hurry."

"Looking round me again, I observed that, quite near my proximity, what I had taken to be a reddish mass of rocks was moving very slowly towards me. Then, to my utter consternation, the bizarre animal was really a monstrous combination of a kind of lobster-crab. Can you imagine a crustacean as large as yonder table, with its many legs moving slowly and uncertainly; its huge claws menacingly swaying; its long antennae, like carters' whips, waving and feeling, and its stalked eyes gleaming at you on either side of its metallic-like front? Its hard-shelled back was corrugated and ornamented with ungainly bumps, and a greenish incrustation blotched the creature's mind-boggling frame, here and there. I could see the many hideous palps of its complicated maw opening, then closing, and feeling around as the hideous thing moved along."

"As I stared at this sinister form crawling towards me, I felt a tickling sensation upon my cheek as though a common housefly had landed there. I tried to brush the annoying irritation away with my right hand, but in a moment, it returned, and almost immediately came another of the weird species by my ear."

"I struck at that feeling, and my hand caught something threadlike that was drawn swiftly out of my hand. With a frightful qualm, I turned, and my alarmed eyes saw that I had grasped the antenna of another monster crustacean that was avariciously crawling-around just behind me. Its evil eyes were wriggling upon their primitive-looking stalks, and its mouth was all alive with appetite; my eyes noticed its vast ungainly claws, smeared with an algae slime, and its grabbers were hungrily descending upon me."

"In a moment, my nervous right hand was again upon the dashboard lever, and soon, I had placed a month between myself and those dreadfully weird monsters. But I was still stationed upon the same beach, and I saw the odd creatures distinctly as soon as I stopped. Dozens of the species seemed to be crawling in circles here and there, in the somber light, maneuvering among the foliated sheets of intense green."

"I cannot convey the sense of abominable desolation that hung over the visible world. The red eastern sky; the northward blackness; the salt Dead Sea; the stony beach infested with these foul, slow-stirring monsters; the uniform poisonous-looking green of the lichenous plants; the thin air that hurts one's lungs: all of those outlandish perceptions contributed to completing a most appalling effect."

"Being excessively worried, I grabbed the forward control and moved-on another hundred-years, and there was the same red sun, a trifle larger, and a little duller; the same dying sea; the same chilled air, and the same crowd of unearthly crustacea meandering in and out among the green weeds and the red rocks. And in the westward sky, I glimpsed a curved pale line, very dark like a tremendously vast second moon."

"So, I traveled ahead, stopping ever and again, in great strides of a thousand years or more, drawn-on by the mystery of the dying Earth's fate, and watching with a strange fascination the sun growing larger and duller in the westward sky, as the life of the old Earth gradually ebbed away."

"At last, more than thirty-million-years hence, the huge red-hot dome of the sun had come to obscure nearly a tenth of the dark heavens. Then, I stopped once more, for the crawling multitude of lobster-crabs had disappeared, and the red beach, save for its livid green liverworts and lichens, seemed positively lifeless. And now, to my dizzy mind, the same beach was flecked with white accumulations. A bitter cold soon assailed me. Rare-but-huge white flakes, ever and again, came sprinkling and eddying-down, signifying the perilous start of a devastating Ice Age."

"To the north-eastward, the intense glare of snow lay under the starlight of the sable sky, and I could see an undulating crest of hills converting their reflection to pinkish-white. There were now fringes of thick ice along the sea margin, with drifting masses, yes, miniature icebergs, farther out; but the main expanse of that salt ocean, all bloody under the eternal sunset, was still relatively unfrozen."

"I looked about my' vantage point to see if any traces of animal life remained. A certain indefinable apprehension still kept me seated in the saddle of the Time Machine. But I saw nothing moving, on Earth, or sky, or sea. The green slime upon the shore rocks alone testified that primitive life was not yet extinct. A shallow sandbank had appeared in the sea, and the water had receded a hundred yards from the beach."

"I fancied that I had witnessed some black object flopping-about upon the beach's margin, but it became motionless as I briefly stared at it. I judged that my eyes had been deceived, and that the black object was merely a motionless rock. The stars in the sky were intensely bright, and seemed to twinkle and sparkle very little. Indeed, gentlemen. The end of the world to me seemed even more fucked-up than the perpetual pessimism that you so-called professional men exhibit right here in Queen Victoria's England of 1899!"

"Suddenly, I noticed that the circular westward outline of the sun had changed; that a concavity, a bay, had appeared inside the curve. And I observed that the bend was amazingly growing larger. For a minute, perhaps, I peered aghast at this blackness that was creeping over the day, and then I realized that an astonishing eclipse was beginning. Either the moon, or the planet Mercury, was passing across the sun's disk. Naturally, at first impression, I perceived it to be a distant moon, but there is much to incline me to believe that what I really had visioned was the transit of an inner planet, such as Venus, passing very near to the virtually-lifeless Earth."

"The darkness grew wider and greater; a cold wind began blowing in frightening gusts from the east, and the alien, showering white flakes in the air increased in number. From the edge of the sea came a low ripple and whisper. Beyond those lifeless sounds, the pathetic world was silent. Silent? It would be hard to convey the stillness of it all."

"All the sounds of man; the bleating of sheep; the cries of birds; the hum of insects; the stir that makes the recognizable background of our lives; all of that common activity was completely finished. As the darkness thickened, the eddying flakes grew more abundant, wildly dancing before my eyes; and the cold of the air became more intense."

"At last, one by one, swiftly, one after the other, the white peaks of the distant hills vanished into complete and stunning blackness. The cold breeze quickly rose to a moaning wind. I saw the black central shadow of the eclipse sweeping towards me. In another moment, the pale stars alone were visible. All else was rayless obscurity. The dying sky was absolutely black."

"A horror of this great darkness came upon me, and it quelled my spirit of discovery. The cold, which smote to my marrow, along with the great chest pain I felt doing difficult breathing, separately overcame me. I shivered, and a deadly nausea seized my stomach. Then, like a red-hot bow, the edge of the sun appeared in the sky. I stupidly got-off the machine, attempting to recover from my giddy dizziness."

"I had felt incapable of boldly facing the return journey back to 1899. As I stood hunched-over, sick and confused, I noticed again the moving thing upon the nearby shoal; there was no mistake now that it indeed was a moving creature and not a rock illusion, moving slower than a snail against the red sea water. The possible amphibian displayed a rounded mass, the size of a rugby ball perhaps, or, it may be even bigger, and its wriggling tentacles trailed-down from its intimidating form. The scary object seemed black against the weltering, blood-red water, and the weird creature was fitfully hopping-about like a wounded frog. Then, I felt as if I was fainting and ready to go unconscious. But a terrible dread of lying helpless and alone in that remote and awful twilight sustained me, and it compelled my will to clamber-upon the machine's saddle, in order to return back to good old London, England, 1899."

Jay Dubya

Chapter 14

"THE TIME TRAVELER RETURNS"

"So, I came back to 1899, late December, just before New Year's Day, and a new exciting century occurring. For a long time, my thought processes must have been indiscernible while riding upon the gyrating Time Machine. The blinking succession of the flickering days and nights was resumed; the life-giving sun became golden again, and the mauve sky wonderfully became an azure blue. I gratefully breathed with greater freedom. The fluctuating contours of the land ebbed and flowed throughout my return journey. The dials upon the dashboard rapidly spun backward."

"At last, I happily again appreciated the dim shadows of ordinary houses, the evidences of the decadent humanity which I had tried to escape, only to encounter a future scenario that was even much worse. Those fleeting images, too, changed and passed, and others came, marvelously taking their place. Presently, when the millions' dial was at zero, I slackened my speed, preparing to suavely halt."

"I began recognizing our own drab, all-too-familiar architecture, as the thousands hand returned back to its starting-point. The alternating night and day flapped slower and slower. Then, the old walls of the laboratory came round me, and I felt a certain comfort in knowing that I had safely come back to my point of origin. Very gently, I slowed the mechanism-down to fully acknowledge all that was dear to me."

"I saw one little thing that seemed strangely peculiar to my comprehension. I think I have told you that when I set-out on my monumental time voyage, before my velocity became very high, Mrs. Watchett had walked across the room, traveling, as it seemed, to my alert attention, like a zooming rocket. As I returned, I passed again across that particular same minute, when my house-woman had interestingly traversed the laboratory in the opposite direction with her every stride, appearing to be taking the exact inversion of her previous route. 'Mrs. Watchett does not *watch it* happening!' I mentally jested."

"The door at the lower end of my laboratory opened, and my housekeeper glided quietly through the laboratory, and like a female magician, disappeared behind the portal from which she had previously entered. Just before *that* wonder had occurred, I seemed to see my cynical friend, Blank, the newspaper Editor, speed-by the doorway in a flash."

"Then, I expertly stopped the machine, and just before my scheduled arrival for our weekly dinner ritual, my landing had occurred at the opposite wall of the old familiar laboratory; the exact distance being the separation of the little lawn and the bronze pedestal of the White Sphinx."

"My favorite tools, and my assorted appliances, were still lying upon the experimenting table, just as I had left them a week before. I got-off the machine very shakily, and sat-down upon my workbench to reorganize my disheveled mind. For several minutes, I trembled violently, recollecting the memory of losing petite Weena, and also recalling the threat of the diabolical Morlocks. Then, remembering to practice my British 'stiff upper lip' deportment, my demeanor became a bit calmer. I was feeling quite thrilled, because around me was my old workshop, exactly as it had been prior to my departure into the distant future. I might have slept there for several hours inside my laboratory, and the whole adventure having been a fantastic dream, I imagined."

"And yet, not exactly! The Time Machine had started from the south-east corner of the laboratory. But it had come to rest again now in 1899 in the north-west, almost against the opposite wall where you gentlemen had seen it last week. In indisputable mathematical terms, I must reiterate that *that* measurable difference in space gives you the exact distance from the little lawn where I had first landed, to the bronze pedestal of the White Sphinx, into which the animalistic/cannibalistic Morlocks had deviously conveyed my machine."

"For a time, my brain had gone stagnant. Presently, I rose and sauntered through the passage here, feebly limping, because my heel was still painful from my shoe's protruding nail, and to make matters worse, I was feeling sorely begrimed and in need of a bath."

"I saw the latest edition of the *Pall Mall Gazette* upon the table by the door. I found that the newspaper's publication date was indeed today, and looking at the wall's timepiece, I saw that the clock's hour was almost eight p.m."

"I heard your voices loudly conversing, and my ears also discerned the distinct clatter of dinner plates. I hesitated entering, for I felt so sick and weak. Then, I sniffed good wholesome meat, and my bruised hand opened the door to re-visit your' company. Now, my good friends, you know the rest. I washed, and dined, and right this minute, I'm concluding the honest-to-goodness story of my entire Time Travel adventure."

Jay Dubya

Chapter 15

"AFTER THE STORY"

"I know," the Time Traveler declared, after a short pause, "that all this retelling has seemed absolutely unbelievable to you, but to me, the one incredible aspect is that I'm here tonight in this old familiar room, looking into your friendly faces, and divulging to you these strange adventures that must sound like absolute fiction." Our itinerant host then looked at the always-cynical Medical Man. "No. I cannot expect *you* to believe it. Take it as a gaudy lie, or perhaps a phony prophecy. Say that I dreamed the entire fiasco in my workshop, and state that I'm looking for a gullible book publisher. Consider the notion that I've been speculating upon the destinies of our race, until I've hatched this nebulous allegory. Treat my assertion of its truth as a mere stroke of art designed to enhance and embellish its interest," our garrulous host insisted. "And taking its entirety as a regular fiction story, what do you think of its plot and theme?"

Mr. Wells took-up his pipe, and began, in his odd accustomed manner, to tap it nervously upon the bars of the grate. There was a momentary stillness, as no one knew exactly what special words to articulate. Then, chairs began to creak, and shoes started to scrape upon the carpet. I took my eyes off the Time Traveler's face, and looked around at his dubious audience. The other men seated in the dining room were exceptionally quiet and pensive. The Medical Man seemed especially absorbed in his mental evaluation of our host's seemingly fanciful narrative. The newspaper Editor, whose domain was principally expository non-fiction writing, was staring hard at the end of his cigar, the sixth. The Journalist, not used to assessing novels and short stories, fumbled for his watch. The others present in the dining room, as far as I remember, were motionless and rather reticent.

Blank, the Editor, stood-up with a sigh. "What a pity it is you're not an author of stories like William Shakespeare or Charles Dickens!" the skeptic muttered, putting his hand upon the Time Traveler's shoulder, showing his doubting encouragement.

"You don't believe it?"

"Well, it's fantastically inconceivable!"

"I thought not."

The Time Traveler next turned to the remainder of his laconic audience. "Where are the matches?" Wells inquired. Our friend lit one and spoke over his pipe, puffing and then coughing. "To tell you the God's honest truth, I hardly believe it myself. And yet..."

Mr. Wells' eyes fell, displaying a mute inquiry upon the withered white flowers laying upon the little table. Then, the shrewd inventor turned over his hand that had been holding his pipe, and I observed that H.G. was looking at some half-healed scars upon his ten knuckles.

The Medical Man rose from his chair, came to the lamp, and examined the flowers that the Time Traveler had removed from his pocket and had carefully laid upon the dinner table. "The stems and petals are quite odd," the renowned London physician and amateur botanist declared.

The Psychologist leaned forward to examine the flowers, holding-out his hand for a closer inspection of the specimens.

"I'm hanged if it isn't a quarter to one," said the Journalist in the meantime. "How shall we get home? I feel as if I'm sleep deprived!"

"Plenty of cabs at the station," the Psychologist stated and then yawned.

The Psychologist handed the wilted flowers to the Medical Doctor. "It's a curious thing," said the Doctor. "But I certainly don't know the natural order of these flowers. May I have them to take to a botanist expert, a professor, who is a casual acquaintance of mine?"

The Time Traveler hesitated. Then feeling insulted, H.G. suddenly answered, "Certainly not."

"Where did you really get them?" questioned the Medical Man. "At a Polynesian florist shop?"

The Time Traveler put his hand to his forehead, suggesting the onset of a migraine headache. Mr. Wells spoke like one who was trying to keep hold of an idea that was endeavoring to elude his brain. "The odd flowers were put into my pocket by Weena, when I had first traveled into Time."

The T.T. stared round the room to assess our general reactions to his remarkable claim. "I'm damned if it isn't all going to hell in a handbasket. This room, and you, my dubious-minded friends, and the general atmosphere of every day, are presently too much for my memory to fathom. Did I ever make a Time Machine, or even a model of a Time Machine? Or is it all only a vague, illusive dream? Many philosophers say that life is but a dream; a precious poor dream at times, but I can't stand another irregular idea that won't fit. It's all utter madness; near insanity. And where did the dream come from? I must again look at and touch that wonderful machine. If there really is one!"

Mr. Wells swiftly picked-up the lamp, and carried it, flaring red, through the doorway, and into the lengthy corridor. We, like curious disciples, followed our' savant's path. There in the flickering light of the transported lamp was the actual machine, sure enough, appearing squat, ugly, and askew; a marvel of brass, ebony, ivory, and translucent, glimmering quartz. The three-dimensional device was solid to the touch, for I put-out my hand and felt the bent rail, and the impressive apparatus showed brown spots and smears upon the ivory sections; and also, exhibited bits of grass and moss upon the lower parts, and finally, a second rail bent awry.

The Time Traveler gently put the lamp-down upon the workbench, and ran his hand along the mechanism's damaged rail. "It's all right now," H.G. declared with a sigh. "The story I've just told you was true. I'm sorry to have brought you out here into this cold room." Wells then held-up the lamp, and, in an absolute silence, the group solemnly and soberly returned to the warm dining room.

The accommodating Time Traveler came into the hall with us and helped the Editor on with his overcoat. The Medical Man looked into his scarred face and, with a certain hesitation, told our host that he apparently was suffering from extreme overwork, at which "H.G." indulgently laughed. I remember our loquacious 'bard' standing in the open doorway, bellowing "good-night" to everyone in a rather disconsolate and disappointed tone of voice.

I shared a cab into downtown with the Editor, who thought the entire tale to be a "fabricated lie".

"Look Hillyer," Blank imperatively said to me. "That lengthy story we just heard was something between a canard and a farce. The only good thing that I can think of right now is that tomorrow we all get laid?"

"Why is that?" I wondered and seriously questioned.

"Because, tomorrow is fuckin' Friday!" Blank, the empty-headed newspaper Editor, cynically and distastefully joked.

I had always regarded Blank as being an obese, obnoxious, hedonistic parasite. As for my own part, although I admire, trust, and really respect the Time Traveler, I was unable to come to a definite conclusion. His story was so fantastic and incredible, yet its telling had sounded so credible and authentic. In fact, I lay awake most of that night thinking about it.

I determined to go the next day to Richmond and again converse with the Time Traveler. I was informed by Mrs. Watchett that Wells was busy working inside the laboratory, and being on easy terms in the house, I stepped-down the familiar corridor to cordially greet him. The laboratory, however, was empty of any human. I stared for a minute at the Time Machine, and put-out my hand upon the device, and next gingerly touched the right lever. At that, the mass swayed like a bough shaken by the wind. Its instability startled me extremely, and I had a queer reminiscence of the childish days when I used to be forbidden to meddle with what I did not understand.

I came back through the corridor, searching for Wells. The Time Traveler met me in his home's smoking room. In a hurry, the science experimenter carried a small camera under one arm and a knapsack under the other. My preoccupied acquaintance chuckled when he saw my presence, and gave me an extended elbow to shake. "I'm frightfully busy," Herbert George announced, "with that amazing machine stationed in there."

"But is it not some extraordinary hoax!" I exclaimed and gasped. "Do you really travel through time?"

"Really and truly, I do." And then, Wells looked frankly and intently into my eyes. His head surveyed the room as if he was being surveilled by the doubting Editor, or by the dubious Medical Doctor. "I only want half an hour," H.G. whispered to me. "I know why you came, and it's awfully good of you. There are some magazines here for you to peruse in the meantime. If you'll stop to have lunch, I'll prove to you that this time traveling business is quite valid and verifiable, future specimens and all. If you'll have the courtesy to please forgive my leaving you now?"

Feeling very concerned and flabbergasted, I consented to his urgent request, hardly comprehending then the full import of his words. And Wells politely nodded, and soon hustled-on down the drafty corridor. I heard the laboratory door slam, seated myself in a comfortable green leather chair, and picked-up the morning newspaper. 'What was he going to do before lunch-time in less than an hour?' I wondered in amazement.

Then suddenly, I was reminded by an advertisement I was reading that I had promised to meet Richardson, the wealthy publisher, at two. I glanced at my trusty watch, and noticed that I could barely honor that engagement. I stood-up and paced-down the all-too-familiar passage to tell the Time Traveler I had to leave his residence to meet the publisher.

As I took hold of the handle of the door, I heard a distinct click and a loud thud. A gust of air whirled round me when I opened the door, and from within came the sound of broken glass falling upon the tile floor. The Time Traveler was not there. I seemed to see a ghostly, fuzzy figure sitting inside a whirling mass of black and brass for a moment; a figure so transparent that the bench behind him, with its sheets of complicated drawings, was absolutely visible; but that entire swirling phantasm vanished as I vigorously rubbed my eyes."

The Time Machine and its most-clever rider had disappeared. Save for a subsiding stir of spinning dust, the further end of the laboratory was then inexplicably empty. A pane of the skylight had, quite apparently, just been blown-in from the great tumult.

I felt an unreasonable astonishment that transcended my mortal sensibilities. I knew that something totally strange and bizarre had happened, and for the moment, could not distinguish exactly what the weird spectacle might be. As I stood staring, the door into the garden opened, and the man-servant appeared.

We looked at each other, shrugging our shoulders. Then ideas began to come, and words were nervously exchanged. "Has Mr. Wells gone out that way?" I asked.

"No, Mr. Hillyer. No one has come out this way. I was expecting to find him here inside his secret laboratory."

At that verbal interaction, I completely understood the situation. At the risk of disappointing Richardson, I stayed on, waiting for the eccentric Time Traveler; waiting for the second, perhaps still-stranger story, and I strongly desired examining the unique specimens and exquisite photographs that Wells would bring back with him as undeniable proof. But I am beginning now to fear that I must wait a lifetime. The Time Traveler had vanished three years ago. And, as everybody now knows, the inventor has never returned with his aspired Eloi prize, petite, and quite-charming Weena.

Unlike argumentative Filby, and the other principal cynics who had had impatiently heard H.G.'s rather incredible story, I, Henry Hillyer, personally admire and have known the Time Traveler for many years, and being fully aware of his awesome determination, I'm still looking forward to his return to London with vivid descriptions and concrete evidence of his latest adventures, from both the past, and the future.

EPILOGUE

One cannot choose but wonder. Will Wells ever return? It may be that H.G. had swept back into the past, and fell among the blood-drinking, hairy savages of the Age of Unpolished Stone; or maybe the daring fellow ventured into the abysses of the Cretaceous Sea; or perhaps the adventurer is living amongst the grotesque reptilian brutes of the Jurassic Age.

The ambitious Time Traveler may even now be wandering upon some desolate, prehistoric coral reef, or exploring beside the lonely saline seas of the Triassic Age. Or did my friend Wells journey forward, into one of the nearer ages, in which men are still competitive fellows, but with the riddles of our own time satisfactorily answered. Yes, we all have dreams and ideas. But my old friend, Herbert George Wells, had the unique ability to make the idea into the thing; the perfect example of his inimitable genius being the actual creation of the very surreal Time Machine.

It is my suspicion that idealistic Mr. Wells has courageously returned to the age of the Eloi, and his central intent had been to rescue Weena, before the heinous Morlocks had attacked her and him in the spectacular forest fire, and to the intrepid Time Traveler's dismay, the petite girl's fate had become a baffling mystery that must be answered. I believe that the "T.T.", which I often now refer to Wells as a nickname of respect, desired either to live harmoniously with Weena in another more-favorable time period, or eventually bring the sweet girl back to good old Victorian London, England, 1899.

But to my baffled imagination, the future is still black and blank, and is actually a vast ignorance, lit at a few casual places by the memory of his fascinating story. And I have by my side, for my comfort, two strange white, flowers, shriveled, brown, flat and brittle. The unique specimens are both witness and testimony, that to my belief, the unidentified flowers both verify and validate the truthful existence of the Time Machine, and in my mind, the two items confirm the Time Traveler's truly amazing story.

About the Author

Jay Dubya is author John Wiessner's pen name and also his initials (J.W.) John is a retired New Jersey public school English teacher and he had taught the subject for thirty-four years. John lives in southern New Jersey with wife Joanne and the couple has three grown sons. John is the creator of fifty-nine books.

Jay Dubya has written adult satires *Fractured Frazzled Folk Fables and Fairy Farces* and *FFFF and FF, Part II*. *Black Leather and Blue Denim, A '50s Novel* and its sequel, *The Great Teen Fruit War, A 1960' Novel* and *Frat' Brats, A '60s Novel* are adult-oriented literary endeavors constituting a trilogy.

Pieces of Eight, Pieces of Eight, Part II, Pieces of Eight Part III and *Pieces of Eight, Part IV* are' short story/novella collections featuring science fiction, paranormal and humorous plots and themes. *Nine New Novellas* is the companion book to *Nine New Novellas, Part II, Nine New Novellas, Part III* and *Nine New Novellas, Part IV*. And *So Ya' Wanna' Be A Teacher* is a satirical autobiography describing the author's thirty-four-year educational career in American public schools.

Ron Coyote, Man of La Mangia is adult humor and the work is an imaginative satire/parody on Miguel Cervantes' Don Quixote, published in 1605. *Mauled Maimed Mangled Mutilated Mythology* is a work that satires twenty-one famous ancient tales. *The Wholly Book of Genesis* and *The Wholly Book of Exodus* are also adult satirical *humor*. *Thirteen Sick Tasteless Classics, Thirteen Sick Tasteless Classics, Part II, Thirteen Sick Tasteless Classics, Part III* and *Thirteen Sick Tasteless Classics, Part IV* are adult satirical rewrites of famous short fiction.

John has also authored a trilogy of young adult fantasy novels, *Enchanta, Pot of Gold* and *Space Bugs, Earth Invasion. The Eighteen Story Gingerbread House* is a new collection of eighteen diverse and creative children's stories.

Jay Dubya likes '50s rock and roll music and he also enjoys pop' songs by the Beach Boys, Fleetwood Mac, the Eagles, the Rolling Stones, ELO, John Mellencamp and by John Fogerty.

Author Biography

Born in Hammonton, NJ in 1942, John Wiessner had attended St. Joseph School up to and including Grade 5. After his family moved from Hammonton to Levittown, Pa in 1954, John attended St. Mark School in Bristol, Pa. for Grade 6, St. Michael the Archangel School in Levittown for Grades 7 and 8 and then Immaculate Conception School, Levittown, Pa. for Grade 9. Bishop Egan High School, Levittown Pa was John's educational base for Grades 10 and 11, and later in 1960, the aspiring author graduated from Edgewood Regional High, Tansboro, NJ. John then next attended Glassboro State College, where the future author was an announcer for the school's baseball games and also read the nightly news and sports over WGLS, GSC's radio station.

John Wiessner had been primarily an English teacher in the Hammonton Public School System for 34 years, specializing in the instruction of middle school language arts. Mr. Wiessner was quite active in the Hammonton Education Association, serving in the capacities of Vice-President, building representative and finally, teachers' head negotiator for 7 years. During his lengthy teaching career, John had been nominated into "Who's Who Among American Teachers" three times. He also was quite active giving professional workshops at schools around South Jersey on the subjects of creative writing and the use of movie videos to motivate students to organize their classroom theme compositions.

John Wiessner was very active in community service, being a past President of the Hammonton Lions Club, where he also functioned for many years as the club's Tail-Twister, Vice-President and also Liontamer. John had been named Hammonton Lion of the Year in 1979, and in 2009, the community helper earned the prestigious Melvin Jones Fellow Award, which is the highest honor that a Lion can receive from Lions International.

John also was a successful businessman, starting with being a Philadelphia Bulletin newspaper delivery boy for two years in the late 1950s in Levittown, Pennsylvania. After his family moved back to New Jersey in 1959, John worked at his grandparents and his parents' farm markets, Square Deal Farm (now Ron's Gardens in Hammonton) and Pete's Farm Market in Elm, respectively. He later managed his wife's parents' farm market, White Horse Farms in Elm for three summers.

Also, in a business capacity, for 16 summers starting in 1967 John Wiessner had co-owned Dealers Choice Amusement Arcade on the Ocean

City, Maryland boardwalk and also co-owned the New Horizon Tee-Shirt Store for eight summers (1973-'81) on the Rehoboth Beach, Delaware boardwalk. In addition, "Jay Dubya" was a co-owner of Wheel and Deal Amusement Arcade, Missouri Avenue and Boardwalk, Atlantic City. And then, for 18 summers beginning in 1986, John had been the Field Manager in charge of crew-leaders for Atlantic Blueberry Company (the world's largest cultivated blueberry farm), both the Weymouth and Mays Landing Divisions.

After retiring from teaching in 1999, writing under the pen name Jay Dubya (his initials), John Wiessner became the author of 59 books in the genre Action/Adventure Novels, Sci-Fi/Paranormal Story Collections, Adult Satire, Young Adult Fantasy Novels and Non-Fiction Books. His books exist in hardcover, in paperback and in popular Kindle and Nook e-book formats.

Google: Jay Dubya books

www.ingramcontent.com/pod-product-compliance
Lightning Source LLC
Chambersburg PA
CBHW071404120626
46546CB00002B/812